MW01205868

Inside the Body of God

Karen Curry

Indigo Heart Publishing
The Woodlands, Texas

Inside the Body of God

Tradepaper ISBN: 978-0-9827803-4-3

1st Printing November 2008
2nd Printing January 2011
Printed in the United States of America

Table of Contents

Gratitudes

Many thanks to all of my soul mates who have helped me midwife this book; Martin and Connie for always reminding me of my greatness, Aaron, for showing me the beauty of my responsibilities and making me laugh, Meira, who always grounds my mission in such a beautiful way and shares my vision of an abundant world.

The words on these pages would not be here if it wasn't for my beautiful assistant, friend and Earth Angel, Chris, who read every word and celebrated the birth of every chapter and who believed in me long before I believed in myself.

A special thanks to my oldest friend and the father of my children, Kyle, who kept the kids busy while I wrote.

My Guide, Thomas, who has been with me in consciousness since I was four years old, is truly the father of this book and all the courses I teach:

I bow with humility at the feet of my Beloved, who has walked so many lifetimes with me, surrounded me with his love like a cloak, created shelter for my soul and a home for my heart. May he know that I shall always rise up to meet him.

Last, but by no means least, my deepest love and gratitude to my parents who survived raising me and taught me about perseverance and determination (and the power of really bad jokes) and to the five amazing souls, Keegan, Katharina, Karson, Kassidy, and Ayelet, who honor me with the title Mother. Heaven on Earth is their dominion. They are my greatest teachers.

I love you all!

-Karen

I am thankful for the blessing of my Life and all the prosperity that has been bestowed upon me. I am so thankful to be called to share my blessings to help prosper others. Amen.

Introduction

Jesus said, "Let him who seeks continue seeking until he finds. When he finds, he will become troubled. When he becomes troubled, he will be astonished, and he will rule over the All."
-The Gospel of Thomas

We are standing on the brink of a very important time on this planet. We are on the threshold a new era, a New Earth. Prophets from many different cultures and times have spoken of this place metaphorically and literally for thousands of years.

The details of what is to come have been spoken about with vague, frightening words. But the words of the prophets also offer hope and speak to visions of lasting peace on earth, a time of returning to the garden, Heaven on Earth.

We have a choice to accept a time of suffering and destruction or to take the reins of creation into our hands and become the stewards of a new era for humanity. Either way, we play a powerful role in co-creating with God the world we participate in. The real question is which destiny will we choose?

We are already running a default program of destruction. We are always creating and, at this point in time, outer appearances would lead us to believe that we may be on our way to creating our own destruction. Our conditioning through our human experiences on the planet has created, in most of us, a belief that suffering is a part of being human, life is hard and we are here to navigate our way through trials and tribulations so that we can redeem our heavenly rewards when we die.

This deep conditioning creates a matrix for fulfillment into form. If we choose to continue to apply these thought forms, then collectively we will most likely choose an Earth that is fraught with sparse resources, suffering and fighting. Read the paper. The evidence is already building.

But, in this exciting time on the planet, ancient understandings of the human power to create a different world, if we choose, have resurfaced. We are being invited to participate in a new reality that requires us to activate the Divinity within us and to serve as co-creators of a powerful new earth.

Quantum physics has shown us that Light, that which we are all made of, travels in pulses and waves and that, for brief periods of time, two particles of Light can occupy the same space at the same time before diverging onto different paths, creating different destinies.

These points of contact are Points of Evolution, a brief moment when choices and vibrations determine destinies. These Points of Evolution are initiated by chaos, periods of reorganization filled with all kinds of clarifying experiences.

These seemingly chaotic points of pulsing energy, much like the pulses of a womb contracting to birth new life, are actually change points, energized places of choice. Chaos is perceived because in those moments there are an infinite number of paths converging simultaneously

For realities to change, to get off one path and onto a different one, there will be points where the two roads meet. We are at such a crucial junction at this time. The greater the perceived chaos, the bigger the jump between the two roads and the greater capacity there is for growth.

The true purpose of God and the nature of God is growth. God is always seeking, through us, to expand and grow.

We are, right now, being called forth to make a Big Jump. We all intended to be here on Earth at this time to be midwives to this process. We are here to grow.

This is the most exciting time to be here on this planet. We have been preparing for this time forever!

But for us to make the jump in a direction that is joyful and rooted in our consciousness of God, it's going to take a lot of practice and discipline. We are being called upon to release the last threads of belief systems that have kept us separate from our Divinity for lifetimes.

These belief systems are so deep and strong they are rooted into our bodies before we are born. The science of epigenetics shows us that most of our belief systems are patterned within our nervous systems in our bodies by the time we are six years old

The acts of discipline required of us to reprogram our neurobiology have been outlined for us for thousands of centuries. Ancient ones called this discipline Alchemy. Alchemy is not about turning lead to gold literally. This conversion is simply a metaphor about an intentional participation on a journey to creating Heaven on Earth, taking the dark, unformed blackness of lead and turning it into beautiful, deliberately sculpted pieces of art. You are the artist of your life.

The most powerful teachers in any religion have been Master Alchemists. They have manifested water where there was none, fed multitudes with just a handful of fish and a few loaves of bread and won battles with musical instruments, doing the seemingly impossible with their knowledge and faith. These powerful teachers understood that contained within us is the Divine code for creation.

It is time to listen to our teachers and practice the lessons of Alchemy. We are creating the templates for our future right now.

If you are reading this book, then your soul is vibrating with an inner longing to make this world a better place. You desire to feel empowered to make a change in your own life and in the lives of others. My intention is to give you a step-by-step system to help you master the science of Alchemy.

Creation is a logical process. The Universe and God act in an ordered way. In this book I will teach you specific understandings and steps that will help you release the beliefs that make you a "victim" of life. I will teach you to create your own reality, enter into this creative process in partnership with God and ultimately allow for yourself a level of creativity that leads you on a path back to your own magnificent Divinity.

This is a simple process, but not always easy. But the rewards will have a lasting effect for you and leave a legacy for your Earth Brothers and Sisters.

We can manifest a delightful New Earth where all souls remember the infinite power of creation that we carry within us. But we will have to practice the art of Alchemy with discipline..

Before you can get started on the following lessons, there are **13 Key Disciplines** that you must attend to with great consciousness and deliberation. These disciplines take practice, focus and intention.

You will have days when it feels harder than other days. There will be times when you question yourself. This is part of the process and as you go through the lessons, you will learn how to navigate your way through the daily fluctuations of energy.

You are always doing it right. You are always growing and changing and it is truly all good.

13 Key Disciplines

1. Release That Which No Longer Serves You

When your hands are full, you can't open them up to receive something more unless you let something go. We are conditioned to make do with "less than" and to compromise. Everything you see, hear, smell, touch and taste in your outer world is simply a metaphorical representation of where you are at with your Alchemy and consciousness. Your outer world is always talking to you.

If we consciously settle for "less than", then "less than" will show up everywhere in our lives including our bank accounts, our businesses and our relationships.

Now is the time to let go of old habits, patterns, thoughts, actions, relationships, jobs and situations that are no longer in alignment with what you intend to create.

2. Let Go Of Your Past

The past is over. If you allow the stories and excuses from your past to keep you from courageously creating what you want, you are no different than an elephant that is conditioned by the feeling of having a chain around his leg but is actually free to roam.

Do not define yourself by what you have survived. Surviving is less than thriving. Intend to thrive regardless of what has come before. Where you put your focus right now is the template for what is to come.

3. Stay Out Of Doubt

Evolution is happening whether we believe it or not. Think about this. What would people have said in the year 1900 about what is taking place on the planet right now? We are using crystalline and satellite technology to speak to each other all over the world instantly.

I can sit on the beach in California and my daughter can send me a photo of herself brushing her teeth and I can reply with a photo of the ocean and me feeding seagulls. I can check emails instantly from a tiny, hand-held computer that fits in my pocket.

If everything we see, hear, smell, touch and taste is simply a metaphorical representation of our alignment with our consciousness, then our technological advances are simply telling us that we are advancing.

Change is happening. More and more people are waking up and remembering their Divine Magnificence and the power of Alchemy.

You can doubt change and evolution. The truth is that it's going to happen with or without your consciousness. It is Law. We create by thinking and feeling. Do you choose to be a conscious part of the process or do you choose to create by default?

4. Use Fear as Leverage

It's easy to get caught in the sticky web of fear. Fear can create paralysis and feelings of being "stuck". Physiologically we see that the experience of fear can shut down thinking and create a survival reaction.

We mistakenly believe that we are experiencing fear in response to change and respond with conditioned paralysis. But most of us are not really experiencing fear. We are instead experiencing resistance. Real fear protects us. Real fear is your intuition telling you not to do something because it might be life threatening.

For example, your fear might tell you to not go into a dark alley at night. This is intuitive and reasonable.

When you are choosing to not make a change because you are "afraid", you are not really experiencing fear. You are experiencing resistance or a split in your energy. This kind of "fear" is simply your inner, directional compass letting you know that something in the application of your alchemical process is out of alignment.

If you are feeling resistance it is crucial that you ask yourself these two very important questions:

a. Am I really intending what I truly want? Or am I intending what I think I should want, what others want me to want or what I think is possible for me?

b. Do I have beliefs that are keeping me from allowing myself to know that I can have exactly what I intend? For example, do I believe that I have to work hard to make money or that for me to get what I want, I might hurt the people I love?

When you courageously go for what you want...with total honesty and authenticity, no holds barred, no limits...and you believe without a doubt that you can have it, then your resistance magically melts away and you move forward with enthusiasm and great speed.

5. Diligently Tend To Your Vibration

At this point in our evolution, the matrix of time is bending and shifting. Things are speeding up. The time between a thought and its manifestation into form is getting shorter and shorter.

We cannot afford to be lazy in our intentions and thinking. Yes, our neurobiology and our habits make it easy to fall back on old programming. To make change requires consistent application and discipline.

Your mind is an abundant garden. A garden needs good light, soil and water to reach its full potential. Tend to the garden of your mind. Give yourself Light and nourishment to help you maximize the potentials of your dreams.

Educate yourself. Surround yourself with people who support your creative process. Celebrate your successes. Nurture yourself and allow yourself to receive. Delight in your magnificence. Align yourself with your Divinity.

You are an Unlimited Child of God.

The more you practice, the easier it gets. And the easier it gets, the easier it gets.

6. Remember Who You Are and Why You are Here

You are here for a reason. You intended to be here at this time to co-create the future of this world. You are an extremely powerful, unlimited, fully supported Light Being.

You have an important role to play in the evolution of this planet. Each and every one of you has a special job here. In this incarnation, you chose a specific energetic blueprint, your Human

Design, to help you fulfill your life's mission and purpose.

It is crucial that you understand yourself and who you are so that you can continue to create in alignment with the magnificence of who you intended yourself to be.

To learn more about Human Design and to get your free Human Design chart, please visit humandesignforeveryone.com

7. Ask For What You Really Want

You WILL get what you ask for but only if it is what you really want. If you are not courageously asking for exactly what you want, your vibration and intentions won't line up behind it and it won't happen.

So many of us, right now, are walking around frustrated because this "manifesting" thing doesn't seem to be working. If what you are intending isn't really what you are wanting, if your seeming desire is a compromise, an obligation or even if it isn't big enough, you will struggle to get enough energy rolling to create the momentum for creation.

Part of the experience here on the planet at this time is not so much about creating the things we desire as much as it is about creating a vibration of joy and delight and gaining the experience of mastering the power of Alchemy.

We must master Alchemy, as we will be called on to co-create on a global level to change the collective matrix. If we are to collectively choose a destiny for this planet, we have to be experienced conscious creators.

8. Pray For Your Evolution Every Day

This shift on the planet requires discipline. We cannot afford to spend energy focusing on the things, which we do not like about our world, as we know it, or we will create that which we are seeking to eliminate from our experience.

In order to stay aligned on the cutting-edge of consciousness, it is crucial that you set a daily intention to vibrate in alignment with the high vibrations of joy, delight and love. When you pray see yourself manifesting the exact experiences and support you need to help you clarify your intentions and maintain your vibrational alignment with that which you desire.

9. Practice, Practice, Practice

There is no moment in your day or night that is not a spiritual moment. All moments, intentions and actions are spiritual. You are an infinite Light Being experiencing a human perception. This is a small perception of the total aspect of who you really are. It takes practice to live the human life and blend it with the larger aspect of your Divinity.

We are so used to living in a way that is unconscious and haphazard. To implement deliberate, intention-based living takes practice. Alchemy is a new skill and you will have to practice repeatedly.

To be an alchemist is not any different than being a musician. We are all born with the potential to be musicians just like we are all born with the potential to be powerful alchemists. It takes time and practice to make a good musician, just as it takes time and practice to make a good alchemist.

10. Create Community

While making changes in your vibration and mindset ultimately is a personal journey that you must take alone, your outer reality can profoundly influence your inner reality, too. Frequencies modulate. The more you attract and align with others of similar intent and vibration, the faster you will all progress.

This is a time of deep community. We will be called upon to

unite in consciousness to shift our collective beliefs and the collective projection of the planetary matrix. We are not here on this journey to be alone. We are here to create a new world together. We must align ourselves energetically to project vibration of the matrix of Heaven here on Earth.

Now is the time to practice co-creating unified goals and intentions together. When we come together in groups of two or more with the intention to create a deliberate experience we amplify our energies and our opportunities for growth.

11. Be Honest and Authentic

As a creator, you cannot create from a dishonest intention. Your underlying belief and motive for your dishonesty will somehow manifest, usually as chaos. It is Law. You are either going to get caught in your dishonesty because you are afraid of being caught and you focus on it, or you will get caught because your underlying desire is to be authentic.

If your actions and words are not authentic, the truth will prevail. If you are not fully intending what you are saying, there will be no manifestation.

Your ultimate responsibility is to live true to yourself and your desires, with the understanding that when you live true to yourself, you live in alignment with God and your motivations will be to harm no others.

You cannot be responsible for other people's reactions to your truth. You cannot deny who you are or your purpose because of your fear that you may hurt others. You will ultimately hurt them more with your dishonesty. You cannot control the feelings or reactions of others, although you can control your experience of others.

You are perfectly created to assume a role in the evolution of the planet. When you step away from the authentic calling of your soul, you walk away from your potential points of contact that will allow you to create destinies with integrity.

The truth is sometimes when we are not acting authentically, we miss opportunities to evolve and keep others from growing as well. We are not here to be heroes or martyrs. Nor are we here to suffer.

12. Let Go Of the Ropes

For lifetimes we have been conditioned to be prepared, just in case. In the evolving times to come, the cataclysmic nature of potential events may be so unexpected that there will be no preparing.

This is why mastering Alchemy is so vital. When you master Alchemy, you can always use intention and your vibrational alignment to know how to navigate through unpredictable situations.

Alchemy prepares the way for constant and everyday miracles. When you understand the Laws and the physics of the Universe, you know that you can never fall or fail, you are always fully supported and the full blueprint for creation is within you.

Faith and trust are like muscles. They need to be strengthened with exercise and practice. Practice Alchemy until you are a master. Let go and trust that when you are in alignment with your Life Purpose and your Divine Blueprint, you will be fully supported.

13. Be Deliberate and Remember Choice

There is not a single moment when you do not have control over your experience. You may not be able to change actual events. There are some events that have been scripted into your journey since before you got here. But you do have control over how you will experience all circumstances.

If you choose to focus on what you do like and what is good about a situation, difficult as it may be, you will ultimately have a deeply different experience than if you are resisting and pushing against situations.

When the heat is on and your experience seems too challenging and difficult, stop and redirect your focus on what you want to be experiencing, what you desire to feel in the situation and hold your attention and emotions in that place to the best of your ability.

It may seem counter-intuitive at this point but I restate that which you focus on grows. If you want to change your experience, you have to change your focus. Look at the good in your situation and keep your focus on your desired outcome.

It's up to you.

Go forth and prosper. May you use your blessings to prosper and bless others!

Inside the Body of God

The Abundance Manifesto

1. I am a radiant, magnetic Being.
2. Abundance is my birthright and my natural state.
3. I attract everything I desire into my life with effortlessness and ease.
4. I know that unseen loving forces are supporting me constantly.
5. I focus my attention and energy on having exactly what I want manifest in my life.
6. I am fully open to the magic of the Universe helping me with every step of creation. Miracles happen to me every day.
7. I am deeply grateful for all of my life experiences. I know they are helping me expand my thinking and my consciousness.
8. My positive emotions show me that my attention is in alignment with my desires. I am on my way to creating exactly what I want.
9. I surround myself with people who support my creative process.
10. Abundant opportunities are always presenting themselves to me.
11. Creation is a constantly evolving process. I am always doing it right! I am always growing and changing!
12. I take guided actions that are in alignment with my desires and beliefs.
13. I am fully supported, deeply loved and magnificently powerful! I am an unlimited Child of the Universe.

Get Your FREE Prosperity E-Book
http://www.joyfulmission.com/ebooks.html

Karen Curry

Jesus said, "Preach from your housetops that which you will hear in your ear. For no one lights a lamp and puts it under a bushel, nor does he put it in a hidden place, but rather he sets it on a lamp stand so that everyone who enters and leaves will see its light."

-Thomas

Inside the Body of God

20

Chapter One

You are a Radiant Magnetic Being

Over the last few years you may have heard a lot about the Law of Attraction. The Law of Attraction basically states that all your thoughts, all images in your mind, and all the feelings connected to your thoughts create your reality. In other words, everything you have in your life - now - has been attracted to you by you through your thinking, your beliefs and your feelings.

It took me a while to understand that this whole "attracting" process wasn't just about having a thought and "poof" the object of my thought magically appears.

Or somehow locking onto the object of your desire and pulling it towards you with some kind of voodoo tractor beam from Star Wars...

Consciously using the Law of Attraction to create is all about vibrations. You are magnetic, meaning you attract what you focus on. And you are also radiant. In order to magnetize what you focus on, you have to first radiate a vibration that is in alignment or harmony with what you want.

This is a totally natural process and happens all the time, even when you are not conscious of it. Everything in your life right now is there because it is energetically resonant with the vibrations you radiated.

Let me explain.

We live in a world that appears to be solid, dense and very defined. As you read this book, it is sitting firmly in your hands. When you turn the pages, you can feel the distinct aspect of the page in between your fingers.

But the seemingly solid nature of the world is really an illusion, created by the unique combination of quantum physics, our human senses and our thought paradigms. What appears as solid matter is actually mostly air, an illusion hung together perfectly by a bunch of atomic particles vibrating and zooming together.

The book you are holding is made of tiny particles called atoms. Atoms are comprised of a few basic parts. In the center of the atom is a nucleus, which doesn't move very much. Within the nucleus are smaller particles called protons and neutrons.

Everything in the world is made of atoms. Everything.

Atoms are made mostly of space. The particles in an atom, the nucleus, the proton and the neutron are very, very small and rotate around each other with lots of room in between the particles.

Everything in the world, including your own body and the chair you are sitting in, is mostly space. But we perceive it as real and solid.

Vibration is a key element in keeping the illusion of solidity in place. The subatomic particles of the atom move and vibrate so quickly that we do not perceive the space between.

There is vibrational alignment between the atomic particles that hold them together with their nucleus. The subatomic particles are attracted to their nucleus. It is very hard to pull the pieces of an atom apart and when it happens, tremendous energy is released. This is a very simple summary of how atomic energy works.

Different atoms come together to make molecules. Molecules are simply more than one atom connected together.

Specific conditions have to happen for atoms to bind together molecularly. There are very finite, "attractive" conditions that have to exist for atoms to connect together.

All things are made of atoms and molecules. All things vibrate. Even you. Even rocks.

Everything on the planet comes together because of specific attractive forces that determine whether they are a good "match". There has to be vibrational alignment for things to be "attracted" to each other. This is a harmonious process. If there is no vibrational alignment then connection doesn't happen.

In fact, if there is no vibrational alignment then atoms (and everything on the planet) actually repel each other.

Because we are constructed entirely of atoms and molecules, the rules that apply to atomic behavior also apply directly to us as humans.

We exist at a vibrational frequency. We have a base line vibrational frequency that is our natural state of wellness and abundance. We are hard-wired energetically to feel good and experience abundance.

As we experience life on Planet Earth, we are conditioned by our world, our families and friends, collective belief systems and consequent experiences. Our conditioning can affect our base-line vibrational frequency, either raising it or lowering it.

Your consciousness, emotional state and thinking determine your frequency. Your base-line vibration is attracting experiences, people and circumstances that are aligned with your frequency.

As your grandmother may have said, "Like attracts like."

If you are happy, you will attract circumstances into your life that are happy. If you are miserable, you will attract circumstances into your life that are miserable.

Think about this for a minute. Pretend like you are sitting in a sidewalk cafe on a beautiful sunny day. A young woman comes by in a brightly colored dress, a smile on her face, swinging her purse and humming to herself.

Everyone sitting at the cafe stops and looks at this woman as she walks by. (The guy next to you even lets out a low wolf whistle.) (You may, of course, whack him with your purse.) She is attractive.

Now imagine that another woman follows behind the first woman. They are identical twins. But, the second twin is wearing gray sweatpants, her hair is shoved under her baseball cap, she is scowling and walking with her head down.

If I hadn't drawn your attention to her, you wouldn't have even noticed her.

Physically, she is identical to the first woman. But, her energy is low and not as attractive to most of the people in the café.

Now, notice that I said not as attractive to most of the people in the café. She is still attractive. Your ability to attract never goes away. But what you attract can change based on your vibrational frequency.

If this sad, downtrodden woman continues to express that frequency of energy, she will most likely attract people and circumstances into her life that are in vibrational alignment with her energy. ("wrong" men, "wrong" friends, "bad" job, no money.... etc.)

The life and people you surround yourself with are there because there is vibrational alignment between you and the circumstances of your life.

When you change your consciousness, emotional state and thinking, you change your frequency. When you change your frequency, you change the things you attract into your life.

This is a lovely feedback loop. The more you change the things you attract into your life, the more your thinking and emotions are affected and the more you attract what is aligned with your frequency.

So, if you are thinking and feeling "good", you attract "good" experiences and people. The more you notice the good circumstances, the better you feel. The better you feel, the higher your vibration, and more good things are attracted into your life.

The converse is also true. If you are feeling "bad", you are vibrating in alignment with "bad" circumstances and you will attract more situations and people to line up with your not feeling good.

You radiate and you magnetize. Your base-line frequency or vibration radiates at a specific level. As you radiate, circumstances, people and thoughts that vibrate at the same speed are then drawn to you.

The more you focus on what you want, believe you can have it and take actions that are in alignment with creating it, the more you vibrate with what you are wanting. You are, in essence, sending out a signal to the Universe indicating that you would like to be having experiences that line up with your frequency.

As you line up your base-line frequency with what you want, you radiate a matched energy with your desire and you magnetize or attract conditions that line up with your base-line frequency.

Your emotional state and your thoughts create your base-line frequency. When you feel good, you radiate a higher vibration. When you feel bad, you radiate a lower vibration.

Of course, the better you feel, the better circumstances you attract. You then feel even better in response to your better circumstances and magnetize even better circumstances. Or vice versa.

You can learn to control your base-line frequency and deliberately maintain or even raise your vibrational state. What you radiate and magnetize is up to you. You are Divinely powerful and you have control over your experience of your life.

The more you learn how to master your base-line frequency, the more control you have over the quality and experiences of your life circumstances. You will never be a "victim" of your life again.

This is true Alchemy.

Exercises:

1. Off the top of your head, write down the top ten reasons why you don't have everything you desire in your life right now. Now notice how much time, attention and focus you place on those reasons.

2. Write down a positive opposite for your top ten reasons.

Example:

I don't know how to manage my money.

To:

I am an excellent money manager.

3. What things do you want the most in life? When you think about these things, are you clear? Do you believe they can really happen for you? Are you taking actions that will help create them?

4. What did your family think about money and being happy? What were you told about money, work, happiness, relationships, etc.? What are your most profound money memories?

Your answers may help you understand your Abundance Frequency.

Jesus said, "If they say to you, 'Where do you come from?', say to them, 'We came from the light, the place where the light came into being on its own accord and established itself and become manifest through their image.' If they say to you, 'Is it you?', say 'We are its children, we are the elect of the Living Father.' If they ask you, 'What is the sign of your father in you?', say to them, 'It is movement and repose.'"

-**Thomas**

Chapter Two

Abundance is Your Birthright and Your Natural State

Focused Review:

Your thoughts and feelings create a vibration. Your vibration determines the experiences you "attract" into your life.

You are an eternal, infinite Light Being. Your essence fills the Universe. You are the Universe. You are a part of everything in your world and The World. Your expansive awareness doesn't have physical boundaries or even physical form.

But, in your awareness, right now, as you read this book, you are a human being. You chose to come here and experience this unique way of being alive. Nowhere else in the Universe is this kind of opportunity available to us. Being a human is a truly magical and very special way of perceiving yourself as being.

There are a lot of ideas about how we choose to come into our human form. Some say that there are finite number of human bodies and a waiting list of souls who want to enter them. Others say that we condense elements of our soul, slow down the vibration and then manifest a part of our souls as humans.

There are so many mysteries in life and so many things to think about. That's part of what makes the human experience so delightful. When we manifest as humans, we forget a large part of the Bigness of Who We Are. And we spend a lifetime working on consciously remembering Who We Really Are.

While the truth of how we come into bodies may be a question that is, at this time, unanswerable with great certainty, there are other truths that are easier to discover.

Everything in the world in manifested form has an energetic blueprint. Just like we have DNA that tells our cells how to express themselves, the entire world has an energetic "plan" or point of expression that then manifests into form.

We can't stray from the blueprint or the structural framework. Think about it. Birth defects and mutations are located in the DNA. If you are constructing a building, the entire structural framework of the building is defined in the blueprint. Any variations from the blueprint that aren't first worked out on paper will most likely result in structural flaws and eventual collapse of the structure.

Most religions teach that we are Children of God. God created us. We come from God.

But that's not enough. There is a danger with not following through with this thought to its deeper understanding. When we perceive ourselves to be children of some deity outside of ourselves, it gives us all kinds of excuses to not line up energetically with the magnificence of Who We Really Are.

When we see ourselves as "children of God", it is easy to think of ourselves as some young, immature, tiny offspring of some benevolent deity who kind of watches us from Heaven, amused by our naivety. Sometimes, this deity has to come down from Heaven and punish us when we are really bad...you know the story.

And, to get even a little more heretical, when we are these little, tiny "children of God", we can also act with reckless impunity and thoughtlessness with the prospect of being forgiven by an eternally Loving Being. The forgiveness part isn't the problem in that scenario, but the reckless impunity and thoughtlessness is. (I'll explain more later...)

You, as a human, have a Divine Blueprint for your human experience. And, because you truly are a Child Of God, your blueprint is the same blueprint as God's Blueprint. You are a Holographic Representation of the Divine.

The word "hologram" comes from the Greek words, "holos" which means "whole" and "gramma" which means "message". In most religious creation stories, God creates the world with words and sounds. Contained within the world is the "Whole Message" of God.

God and The Universe, the "Whole Message" are contained within you. You are God and you are the Universe. Therefore your expression on this planet is truly unlimited, just as God is unlimited.

Think about it. When your physical form comes into manifestation, it takes two parents to create you so that your body is a "mix" of both parents. But your parents are also "Children of God", and their parents and their parents and their parents...

There is one God, the source of life in this Universe. This one God is the originator of everything we know. Because there is one God, when your soul was manifested into form, it was not a "mix" of two entities but a pure expression of the Divine from One Source.

If you want to look at it from a genetics point of view...and genes are simply the blueprints for the physical illusion of the hologram...we are genetically the same as our Creator. Contained within us and expressing through us is all the potential of God. Because, we, as humans, are also God.

We just forget sometimes.

Now, some people get all crazy and worried that if we are God...and notice I didn't say gods...One God...then we can go about our life experience like little dictators doing whatever we choose, without regard to others. Reckless impunity is the order of the day in this model.

But, we live in an ordered and logical Universe. There is no action without an equal and opposite reaction. There are always consequences to all actions. Nothing happens in a bubble. If you choose to act with reckless impunity, there will be a consequence, an equal and opposite reaction, that will be in direct proportion to your action.

Being a human is a unique experience. As the human expression of God, we have unlimited potential. Coming to Earth as a human is a very powerful and important gift because we have experiences here on Earth that we can have no where else in this Universe.

Earth is the perfected expression of the Divine Concept of Duality. It is the manifested form of opposite energy.

There is perceived "good" and "bad". There is "light" and "dark". There is "Heaven" and "Earth". Earth is one of the rare places where we perceive ourselves, through the duality of our perception on the planet, as being separate from God.

When we are in incarnated form as humans, we forget that we are God and we think of God as this Divinity outside of ourselves. And from that primary illusion, all other perceptions of duality flow.

Earth is a crucible for Divine Growth. The nature of life is to grow. Remember the sine wave. It has to vibrate and undulate. Without undulation, no growth happens and we die.

The duality of life on Earth is vital for the growth of the Divine. We are born here on Earth to live the duality because the dual nature of our perception helps God grow. God, through us, is growing.

And our job is to help God grow.

We help God grow by experiencing the duality of the Earthly experience. The "good" and the "bad" that we perceive are not really "good" or "bad". They are two expressions of the same energy.

Our natural state as Divine Sparks is abundance, health, wellness, joy and love. When you look at how we are physically and energetically "hard-wired", we are physically designed to be well. Our bodies are holographic representations of our Divinity.

When we are not in bodies, we exist, unified, as pure Divine Energy and we perceive our Divinity as being "all good". It is only here on Earth that we, by Divine Design, forget that it is "all good" and sometimes get lost in the seemingly darker perceptions of our earthly experience, and we suffer.

We are not here to suffer. But it is easy to get lost in the duality of the Earth experience. We begin to identify with our perceived "bad" experiences. Even our language reflects this. We "are" sad. We "are" depressed. The difficulty of our Earth experiences causes us to sometimes identify and become the experience, instead of allowing the experience to flow through us.

As Divine Holograms, abundance is our natural state. Abundance is the base-line frequency of our vibrational state. It is only on Earth, that we experience the perception of the opposite.

We didn't come here to "be" poor. We didn't come here to "be" miserable. We come here to experience poverty or misery so that we can use these experiences to expand our clarity about what it means to be abundant and joyful.

We are here to experience these seemingly opposite conditions to help us deepen our awareness and capacity to grow abundance and joy.

It's kind of like this. Imagine that you live in a box. You are surrounded by the walls of the box. When you bump into the walls, it helps you define the parameters and the conditions of your box.

After you spend some time in the box, you might decide that you want a bigger box or you want to get out of the box. You wouldn't know what you wanted if the walls of the box didn't define for you what you didn't want any more.

The seemingly negative experiences we have on Earth only serve to deepen our understanding of how and what we want to grow in response to our experience.

The worse our experience, the bigger our understanding and our capacity to grow.

The trick is to not stay in the negativity of the experience. We ARE NOT our experience. We are EXPERIENCING our experience. It is simply happening. It is not who we are.

Who we are is abundant, holographic, unlimited representations of God.

Abundance is our birthright and our natural state.

Exercises:

1. When you think of being abundant without limitations, how do you feel? What thoughts, emotions and images come up for you? Write them down.

2. How do these thoughts, emotions and images influence your current experience of abundance?

3. Are you blocking yourself from creating abundance in response to your unwanted conditions? Do you feel stuck or trapped in conditions that you feel you have no control over?

4. What conditions in your life do you NOT want right now? How are these experiences helping you understand what you DO want?

Jesus said, "If you bring forth what is within you, what you bring forth will save you. If you do not bring forth what is within you, what you do not bring forth will destroy you."

-Thomas

Chapter Three

You Attract Everything You Desire with Effortlessness and Ease

---

Focused Review:

Your thoughts and feelings create a vibration. Your vibration determines the experiences you "attract" into your life.
You are naturally abundant. Abundance is your natural vibration.

"To know the mechanics of the wave [vibration/oscillation] is to know the entire secret of Nature."
-Walter Russell

The Essence of the Divine is within you. That means that you have the ability to create in an unlimited way. You're already doing it, whether you're aware of it or not.

No matter how challenging certain aspects of your life may seem right now, you have the ability to easily and effortlessly turn them around. You can, with a little training, learn how to create exactly what you want in every aspect of your life.

Your ability to create is inherent within you. But, our experiences on Earth make it difficult to remember how powerful and creative you really are.

In Judaism it is said that all babies, prior to birth know the Torah (the Word of God). At birth, God gently thumps the baby on the philtrum (the dent on the upper lip) and the baby forgets everything.

The purpose of forgetting our Divinity, in this story, is to deliberately re-awaken and remember the Divine within us with great consciousness. Although there is such beauty in the innocence of a child who remembers their Divinity, there is an enormous amount of power and appreciation in an adult who consciously calls on their Divinity and commits to remember and act as the God Within.

So, with a toolbox full of creative potential, you have what it takes to re-awaken your Divine Creative Abilities and powerfully live the life you were created to live.

Divine Creative Potential is strong and always creating. You are always creating. You have always been creating. Everything in your life right now is there because you created it. You just might not be aware of exactly how you created it.

Your thoughts are the most powerful creative energy you have at your disposal. What you think about, especially with great consistency, will manifest in your life. It's kind of like your mind is a big magic wand.

But, you have to learn how to use the magic of your thinking. Until you learn how to master your thinking, you will be an untrained "Source"-rer and the conditions of your life will be created by default, or at least without deliberation.

Think about this. Take a minute to write down the top ten reasons you don't have what you want in your life right now. Just go with what comes to you. Don't think too much.

Now, think about how much time you spend thinking about or paying attention to those reasons.

For example, let's say you wrote down that the reason you can't get ahead in your business is because you don't have any money. How much time do you spend worrying, obsessing, thinking and, sometimes, even being afraid of, not having the money you need to grow your business?

Your thoughts are the creative lightning bolts that come out of your magic wand. Until you master the use of your magic wand, you randomly fire creative lightning bolts from your wand and create all kinds of crazy things in your life, some "good" and some "bad".

Creation is happening all the time. It's effortless and easy. The trick is learning how to control your magic and use your creative potential with great deliberation.

Part of why the creation process is so easy is that we have physiological "hard-wiring" within our nervous system that makes creation an effortless process. Our nervous system is designed to make repetitive experiences somewhat "mindless".

Have you ever watched a baby learn to walk? Normally takes two or three months. First, the babies learn to pull themselves up on the furniture. Then, they learn to "cruise" around the furniture, holding on to the edge as they move about. Eventually, they move from couch to chair or chair to table, kind of lunging in the direction they want to go.

Finally they take a step or two, until before you know it, they are walking and then running.

We all go through this elaborate process in some way. Think

about this. When you are walking are you consciously saying to yourself, "Right...now left...now right...now left..."

Hopefully not.

We can walk with little conscious awareness because as we were learning to walk, our nervous system was building a "nerve highway" known as a neuropathway. A neuropathway allows information to travel quickly within the nervous system without a whole lot of conscious thought. So, now when you walk, nerves are firing and sending messages and you are walking...while chewing gum, thinking about life, having an engaging conversation or noticing the handsome man across the street.

It takes twenty-one days of consistent repetition to build a neuropathway. Neuropathways only grow with lots of repetition over time. So, with consistent action, your body makes a neuropathway. Once a neuropathway is built, repetitive thoughts and even actions can happen without a whole lot of conscious awareness.

This is great when you think about walking. But kind of sobering when you think of how effortless it is for you to fire creative thought forms from your magic wand that are not the thoughts you would like to be creating with.

The science of epigenetics shows that when we are conceived our neuro-biology is pretty much a blank slate. We are unlimited in our expression. But, only until we are conditioned by the outer world and collective consciousness, common beliefs held by your world around you.

Research shows that we receive a majority of our conditioning on a cellular level from six months prior to birth until six years of age. That means that most of your beliefs about the world are structured into your nervous system as neuropathways before you may even have conscious memories of being alive.

This starts a very interesting cycle that only serves to deepen your conditioning and promote the evolution of even more neuropathways.

Let's look at this. Let's say you grew up in a family that had strong beliefs that money was something just for lucky people and in "your family" you only have money if you work hard for it.

Beliefs are thoughts that are repeated over time. So, in terms of your magic wand, if you have a conditioned belief that is ingrained in your neuro-biology, your magic wand is repeatedly firing a lightning bolt that carries the energy of your belief.

As your wand repeatedly sends out this message, you are, essentially, sending out a vibration that is in alignment with experiences that reflect this belief. So, going back to your family's belief about having to work hard to make money, you begin to manifest situations in your life that reflect this belief.

As a result, you only make money when you work hard. So you work hard at making good grades and you get rewarded. Maybe you sell lemonade, have a dog-walking business or baby-sit to make money for your upcoming school field trip. You never have more money than you need, just what you earned and worked hard for.

Of course, as your outer world begins to reflect what you created with your magic wand, your biology continues to collect data to support your belief system and the belief becomes more deeply rooted in your conscious awareness and, of course, your neuropathways.

What that means is that, with very little attention and effort, your mind is sending out signals to the world via a neuropathway, and you are effortlessly and easily creating whatever it is that you are radiating out from your mental magic wand.

It takes time and consistent repetition to create a new neuropathway. Until you have a new neuropathway built, your neuro-biology will always fall back on the old neuropathways as the default position.

This is why you can go to a workshop or training, come away all fired up, do all the new things that you learned for a short period of time. But, when your circumstances prove challenging or don't appear to be changing fast enough, the old thought patterns and habits return. You unconsciously run your default program.

Many people feel badly when they fail to make a change and worry that they have character flaws, "blocks" or weaknesses. If you have failed to make significant changes, even if you "know" better, it is more likely that you have simply lacked a basic understanding of how you operate as a human.

It is an unlimited Universe and we are unlimited beings so I will never say that One Minute Miracles are impossible. But, they are not that common.

Most people have to diligently work to change their neuro-biology. It makes sense. If the programming were easy to overwrite, then simple things like walking could easily be forgotten. We have survived and evolved as advanced neurological beings in a way that promotes survival. Your neuro-biology is not your enemy. You just have to really work at it over time and with consistency.

Once you do build new neuropathways and you deliberately radiate the magical messages that vibrate with what you really want for your life, then your creation process becomes truly effortless and easy.

As you consistently radiate new messages, your outer world gradually begins reflecting new conditions and experiences that are in alignment with your deliberate way of thinking.

Of course, as your outer reality begins to reflect your new way of thinking, you deepen the conditioning of your new neuropathways and your creation process becomes more and more effective.

Isn't it amazing that your physiology is designed for creating in an effortless and easy way? With just a little re-training, you can get your body, your soul and your consciousness to work in alignment and your creation experience will speed up significantly.

Exercises:

1. Write a few paragraphs about what you would like to create in the following six areas of your life:

a. Your health
b. Your finances
c. Your career/creative fulfillment
d. Your relationships
e. Your spiritual connection
f. Your lifestyle and living circumstances

2. Write powerful, affirmative statements that support the creation of your new desires.

For example: I easily create the abundant income I desire. I am a great provider, a prudent investor and a patient saver. I am deeply wise about money and finances. I am excited to have more money in my life!

Write your affirmative thoughts on a 3x5 card. When you are conscious of your non-supportive, old conditioning, pull out your card and read it until you feel the truth of the statement in your heart and solar plexus.

3. Create a visual reminder of your new way of thinking. Make a collage and use visual images that reflect your desires and new beliefs.

You can also make a PowerPoint presentation of your dreams and upload them into your MP3 player. I do this and watch the "movie" of my dreams while I work out on the treadmill. It is also the screensaver on my computer.

4. Find music that inspires you. I like music from www.successmusic.com. Play this music while you are focusing on your new thoughts. When you hear "your" music, it will trigger in you new and powerful ways to think and feel your dream.

Jesus said, "The angels and the prophets will come to you and give you those things you already have."

-Thomas

Chapter Four

Unseen Loving Forces
are Supporting You Constantly

Focused Review:

Your thoughts and feelings create a vibration. Your vibration determines the experiences you "attract" into your life.
You are naturally abundant. Abundance is your natural vibration. Your creative powers work easily and effortlessly all the time. It is your job to direct them.

You are never alone.

You are always surrounded by Unseen Loving Forces. Sometimes we call them Angels, Spirit Guides, Totems, Fairies, crossed over Loved Ones and more.

When you experience an encounter with an Unseen Loving Force, it can profoundly change your life and understanding of reality. Most religious teachings are filled with stories of people who have initiating experiences with Unseen Loving Forces.

Some people report having real experiences of being "helped" by an Angel or mysterious stranger who then disappears. Others can see or hear Unseen Loving Forces and delight in the hidden loving life that surrounds us constantly.

It is a loving Universe and we are not here to suffer. There are legions of Unseen Loving Forces here to help us remain conscious of our abundant birthright.

But, if you contain within you the complete Hologram of God and you have within you unlimited creative potential, and your whole life experience is really a movie generated by you, then who are these Unseen Loving Forces? Who are these mysterious, wise guides who seem to know so much more than we do, give us crucial pieces of information when we need it? (And sometimes even boss us around in a loving way?

They are YOU.

You are your Spirit Guides, your Angels and the Unseen Loving Forces. They are aspects of yourself.

This understanding can be a little challenging, but knowing that even your Inner Guidance is just an aspect of yourself will help you really grasp the extent of your true power and wisdom. When you understand how truly powerful and infinite you are, you will radically unleash your creative potential.

You previously learned that you are a holographic representation of the Divine. The creative potential of God resides within you. As stated so beautifully in Genesis, "Let us make Adam (a representative) in a form worthy of Us (God) as is commensurate with being in Our likeness…"

Your humanness is simply a metaphorical 3-D expression of God. Think about the human body. Within each cell is the potential for the full expression of physical man, your DNA. Every cell contains within it the possibility of manifesting all the parts of the human body.

But, in a human body, each cell is differentiated, each with a unique role and purpose in maintaining the integrity of the human form. Heart cells rhythmically work together to pump blood. Red blood cells carry oxygen to the body. Nerve cells carry the electrical impulses of the nervous system.

And, even though within the center of the cell all parts of the whole can potentially be manifested, the beauty and magnificence of each cell is in the expression of its unique role in maintaining the whole. Each cell helps express the full abundance of the body when the cell carries out its unique and important role.

We are like cells in the God-Body. Each one of us is unique and powerful in the full expression of ourselves. Our greatest responsibility to the Whole is to live out the fullest expression of our potential. When we do our best at being ourselves, we ultimately act for the greater good of the Whole.

Our role in the God-Body is to generate Desire and deliberately experience life. Our job of being consciously aware and generating desire is the driving force that facilitates the growth of the Divine. Our experiences as humans, "good" or "bad", generate desires in response to the experiences. These desires are the leading edge of Divine Consciousness and, through our quest for growth, God grows through us.

Our job is to experience more and want more.

And to help facilitate our journey, we have "helpers" who support us, inform us and remind us of who we are and why we are here. Our Angels, Spirit Guides and other Guides are differentiated energies created to help us along with our experience.

Much like a blood cell is a cell with a specific job in your body, your Guidance "Team" is differentiated Divine Energy with the specific job of helping you on your life path.

These differentiated energies have different frequencies and your own vibrational frequency and intention will create the kind of interaction you choose with your Guidance "Team". Some people seemingly have more natural experiences with their Angels and Guides. Others have to work through their thinking processes to allow themselves to have the pleasure of knowing their Angels and Guides.

There are a few fast and hard rules about connecting with your Angels and Guides. If you want to connect with your Guidance, the most important thing for you to do is to want to be connected. Your intention to connect is the key to unlocking the door that may be keeping you from fully consciously accessing the support that is so readily available to you.

Angel and Spirit Guide energy is high-frequency energy. These are non-incarnated energies so they vibrate on a high level by nature. You will have an easier time connecting if you maintain an open, playful mindset. Remember, these energies are not having an Earth experience so they often won't take your experiences as seriously as you do. Feelings of frustration will make it more difficult for you to perceive these energies.

Your brain has two halves or hemispheres. Your left hemisphere is deeply rhythmic, pattern-based and suspicious of new information until it is proved (over time) to be verifiable. Your right hemisphere is holistic and expansive in its function. Your right hemisphere is the antenna that connects you to Super-Consciousness and the Unseen Loving Forces.

We use both parts of our brains. The left hemisphere helps us understand Earth information. The right hemisphere helps us process guidance and inspiration. We need both parts in order to function effectively on the planet.

The right hemisphere is the part that allows you to connect with your Spirit Guides and Angels. The right hemisphere is deeply connected to emotions and is lacking in suspicion. The more you can playfully engage with your desire to see Angels, Spirit Guides and other Elements of Disincarnate Realms, the easier it is for you to really connect with your Guidance.

When you are trying to connect, if you find that you are taking it way too seriously or you are feeling frustrated that this is just not happening for you, please quit and come back to it later. The truth about frustration is that the more you feel frustrated, the more frustrated you become and, of course, the less likely it is that you will experience the connection you desire.

You are already always connecting with Unseen Loving Forces. In order to consciously connect, you have to learn how to recognize the guidance that you are constantly being given. Once you feel comfortable with the method and cadence of your Guidance, you will understand how your Inner Wisdom and Infinite Self has always been directing and supporting you.

Remember, you are never alone.

There are four common channels that we use when we are receiving guidance from Unseen Loving Forces. We tend to prefer to receive information on one specific channel, although a few of us will receive on all four channels at different times.

Clairvoyance: When you experience clairvoyant intuition, you are "seeing" intuitive information and guidance. For some people that can be an experience of literally seeing visions with the physical eyes but that is unusual.

For most people who are clairvoyant, intuitive sight happens inside the head. Close your eyes for a moment. Now imagine the space between your eyes on the inside of your head is a giant movie screen.

Imagine a flower on the top of a hill, blowing in a gentle breeze, the other long pieces of grass around it bending in unison…

Can you see it?

This is your mind's eye, your clairvoyant sight.

For many of you, when you meditate and connect with your Inner Wisdom, you will have visions or see inside of your head almost as if you are imagining things with your mind's eye.

Claircognizance: This can be one of the more frustrating ways to experience connection with Unseen Loving Forces, especially if you are a very logical person. Claircognizance is intuitive knowingness. When you are claircognizant, you know things, like your Angels may tell you to take a left and you just know that it's correct.

You just know and you don't know how you know. You just know that you know.

If you are a linear thinker, this kind of intuitive connection can drive you nuts. If you are struggling with trusting your knowingness, play with it and see what happens. Start noticing how many times you are right.

The more you notice how right you are, the easier it will be for you to trust it.

Clairsentience: We have a lot of expressions for clairsentience in our culture. Sometimes we call it a "gut feeling" or a "hunch." Clairsentience is when you "feel" intuitive information.

Sometimes it can feel like chills running down your spine or your arm. Sometimes your body will get a specific feeling that tells you that something is "up".

We also call this channel empathy. When you can "feel" someone else's emotional energy or someone else's physical distress in your own body, this is clairsentience.

Clairaudience: This intuitive channel is simply hearing intuitive information. How many times have you heard a voice in your head telling you to do something or even NOT do something?

You may have experienced clairaudience when you have been faced with a potentially dangerous situation. It is common to hear a directive voice telling you something simple like, "get out" or "run", when you are in danger.

Many of you have a constant intuitive voice running through your head. The key to connecting with this voice is making sure that you spend some time in silence each day. Daily meditation is a powerful way for you to quiet yourself and open up to hearing your Inner Voice.

Everyone has Angels and everyone has Spirit Guides. Not having Angels and Spirit Guides would be the equivalent of having a body without blood cells or a heart. These Disincarnate Energies are a crucial part of your Infinite Self and you need them to function. You might not always have been aware of them but they have always and will always be here for you.

Unseen Loving Forces are supporting you constantly!

Exercises:

There are other ways to receive intuitive information. Everyone is unique and you may have your own way of experiencing your Inner Wisdom. These techniques can help you connect with your Unseen Loving Forces. Use them and feel free to change them and make them your own if necessary.

1. Sit silently for 20 minutes in a very comfortable chair. Before you begin to sit in silence, write down the following statement on a piece of paper or in your journal:

"I intend to connect deeply with my Angels, Spirit Guides, Animal Guides and any Unseen Loving Force that is here to help, support and guide me for my highest good."

When you are done listening, write down any insights, thoughts or visions you may have experienced.

2. Sometimes it can be easier to connect with Unseen Loving Forces when you write. This exercise will take about 20 minutes. You will need a blank journal or notebook, a good pen and a quiet space. Take some nice deep breaths and write the following statement at the top of your page:

"I intend to connect deeply with my Angels, Spirit Guides, Animal Guides and any Unseen Loving Force that is here to help, support and guide me for my highest good."

Then write down any question you may have about something going on in your life right now. Then write down the answer.

At first, as you write the answer, you may think you are writing the response but as you write, listen to the voice in your head and read the words you are writing. You may notice that you are writing faster than you would normally and you are having a difficult time keeping up or that the words you are using are unfamiliar. Some people even report that they feel their pen take on a life of its own.

Read your answer. Is it wise and deeply knowing? This process, known as channeled writing, is a powerful way to connect with your Unseen Loving Forces, especially if you have a lot going on in your mind and you have a lot of mental chatter. Writing can sometimes cut through all the noise in your head and give you a clear answer when you are in need of guidance.

3. Go to your local bookstore or metaphysical shop and pick up a deck of oracle cards. Pick a deck that feels good to you and has pictures on it that you resonate with.

Do not read the deck according to the instructions. When you learn to use oracle cards the "right" way, it can become a mental exercise and not a heart-based exercise.

Ask the cards a question and ask that your Unseen Loving Forces help you get the answer you seek.

Lay out the cards in a way that feels correct for you and then ask your Unseen Loving Forces to help you understand the answer.

****

In all of these exercises, pay attention to how the answers sound in your head. You are always receiving information from your Infinite Self and Unseen Loving Forces. With practice, you will be able to "hear" your Guidance all the time and you will know on a deep level that you are never alone.

Jesus said, "Whoever believes that the All itself is deficient is himself completely deficient."

-Thomas

Chapter Five

You Focus Your Attention and Energy on Having Exactly What You Want Manifest in Your Life

----

Focused Review:

Your thoughts and feelings create a vibration. Your vibration determines the experiences you "attract" into your life.

You are naturally abundant. Abundance is your natural vibration. Your creative powers work easily and effortlessly all the time. It is your job to direct them.

You are supported on your Earth Journey by specialized Loving Forces who guide you and give you information to keep you focused on the maximum expression of your soul.

Your mind is a powerful magic wand. The lightning bolt that you "shoot" from your wand is energized by your thoughts. Thought energy is the energy that holds a vibration and aligns you with the reality that you want to experience.

Learning to use a magic wand takes practice. Being deliberate with your thoughts also takes practice. As you have already learned, your physical body and nervous system is designed to make repetitive thought processes rote and "mindless".

You have thought patterns happening in your head all the time. Many of them are simply well worn neuropathways that you have developed over time as a result of your conditioning and experiences in life.

For example, if you were raised in a family who believed that you have to either be born rich or lucky to have money and you had experiences that made this belief seem true to you over time, you probably have a consistent, unconscious thought pattern that gets triggered every time you see a "lucky" wealthy person who happened to be born into the "right" family.

Of course, according to the energy that your mind is radiating, you are aligning with a reality filled with "lucky" wealthy people who are "born rich" and you, being "unlucky" and born into "just enough" keep having "unlucky, just enough" kinds of experiences.

There are no exceptions. You do not create by accident. Everything in your life is there because you aligned with it vibrationally. Everything.

This can feel like bad news but it's actually very empowering news. If you lined up with the reality you perceive right now, then you can align with a different reality and change your life's circumstances.

You are absolutely free to align with any kind of experience you desire. It is, after all, an unlimited Universe with an infinite number of potential realities.

In order to truly understand the power of your thinking, it is vital that you understand more deeply how your brain operates.

Your brain and nervous system have a very important role. Your brain translates your personal Divine Blueprint into a human experience.

The brain has two halves called hemispheres. Divine Inspiration and Information is received, non-verbally in the right hemisphere. The left hemisphere translates these images and impulses into language and actions. The right hemisphere is the receiver and the left is the transformer.

Both parts of the brain are vital, although we have a collective tendency to focus primarily on the left hemisphere creating a society that is very linear, patterned and logical. The left-brain is very focused on "how" we do things. For centuries we have lived in a world that strengthens and nourishes our left hemisphere.

The way we were taught in school, the way we work, the way we are trained to use information is rooted in the left hemisphere. While the left hemisphere is vital, when we use it exclusively, we are left with thinking that is very dense, lacking in emotion and somewhat uninspired.

Without a balanced right hemisphere, there is no real guided action, just random action that is not guided by Divine Inspiration. The right hemisphere receives Divine Inspiration. It is rooted in intuition, gut feelings, expansive and holistic awareness and emotions. When we are right brain dominant, we are not "grounded" in our creations and our actions lack focus and direction. Right brain dominance without a left-brain translation makes getting things done on Earth very difficult.

Both hemispheres are vital. We live in an era when balanced use of both halves of the brain is crucial for Divine Power and Creation.

There are two kinds of thoughts, Divine Thought and human thinking. Divine Thought is unlimited. It doesn't worry about "how" things are going to happen. When Divine Thought happens it is fast, quick and inspirational. As humans, we sometimes experience Divine Thought as a flash or "ah-ha".

When you receive Diving Thoughts, your emotions will align with the thought. Divine Thought feels good and exciting. The prospect of fulfillment of the Divine Thought into action is enlivening and joyful.

Divine Thought feels good. Divine Thought is the blueprint inspiration that lets you know that you are on the right path to fulfill your soul's intention. Divine Thought feels like desire. The desires you have are the whisperings of God in your heart. The desires you have that excite you and feel good are merely the "compass of your soul" letting you know that this is the direction your expanded Self wants you to go in.

It is vital that you feel desire and that you allow yourself to want more and bigger things and experiences. These desires are simply the expansion of God growing through you and they are part of your experience as a human. Without desires, no growth happens, both on a personal and a Divine level.

Of course, desire is always happening. But the translation of the desire into action in the left hemisphere is where we can stumble a bit in our human experience. The second kind of thought, human thinking, is much smaller by nature. Our human minds are charged with the task of translating the unlimited inspiration of the Divine into 3-D human action.

Our human thinking is only seemingly smaller or more limited because of our collective experiences here on Earth. We project thoughts over time that clearly define what is "possible" in our bodies and our life experiences that make us sometimes scoff at our own Divine Inspirations.

For example, in an unlimited Universe, it is conceivable that we could manifest an apple out of pure air into the palm of our hands. But our logical, left-brains tell us that creating an apple out of thin air is "impossible" and wouldn't we be far better served to simply go to the grocery store and buy an apple?

Or, in an unlimited Universe, it is quite possible that you could align with the vibration of a million dollars and manifest that magnificent sum of money overnight. But your logical, left hemisphere struggles to translate the possibility of that happening based on your experiences and beliefs. If you can't believe it, it won't happen.

God within us inspires us, but our human thinking limits the limitless possibilities. This key point is the source of a huge spiritual disconnect that happens on the Earthly plane and keeps us from collectively living "Heaven On Earth".

If we can't imagine "how" something is going to happen, we discount it or even push the experience away by focusing the power of our thoughts on the "impossibility" of the inspiration coming into form.

The sense of "impossibility" is the cause of so much of our perceived human suffering, and spiritual confusion. We are born with a deep understanding of "unlimited possibility." Think about a four-year-old writing a Christmas List for Santa Claus. The list goes on and on...I want a pony, a truck that shoots fire, real spider webs that can shoot out of my fingers like Spider Man, a kitten, three hamsters, enough candy for a whole year that I can share with all my friends....

As children we believe that anything is possible until we are told over and over by our conditioning field that we have to be "realistic" and to not be "greedy" or "selfish" by asking for too much or for things that cost money and are impossible to have.

This isn't intended to be criticism against our parents, loved ones and teachers. They did not intentionally cut us off from our Divinity. They were simply living out their own conditioning and serving to perpetuate the delusion of a separate God and a limited world. We all play a role in continuing this myth.

But, you incarnated at this very important time on Earth to shatter this myth. You chose to be here because it is now time on Earth to fully proclaim our Divine Birthright and live out the nature of God in its full limitless form in the third dimension. This is a tremendously exciting time to be alive and you have a key role in waking up the planet.

Many of you feel a deep frustration in the core of your being. Many of you have been fighting the collective myth of an "impossible" world here on Earth. You may have been searching for a long time for confirmation that you can, indeed, have anything and everything you want...

For your highest good and the highest good of all those who are impacted by your desires...remember, you living out the fullest expression of the magnificent Self you were created to be is the greatest service that you can give to God.

To set ourselves free from the limits imposed on our own Divinity by our human thinking, we have to rewire our brains and remove the collectively imposed shackles that we have placed on our understanding and acceptance of unlimited possibilities.

Sounds like a big task, but it can be easily done, by being disciplined and consistent with your thoughts. With a little time and practice you can reclaim your Divine Power and align yourself with whatever reality you choose to experience...no limits!

If we are indeed created in the likeness of God, and the God Mind is unlimited, then we can also experience unlimited thinking and all possible realities become potential realities for us. Everything is possible if you think it is.

You are not given a desire or inspiration that you are not intended to experience. Remember, the inspiration you experience is the compass of your soul. If it excites you and delights you, then it is in alignment with your natural abundant state and you simply need to learn how to turn the inspiration into a "real" experience.

Your mental "magic wand" translates inspiration into a creative vibration through focused intention.

We call this the Law Of Focused Success:

**Where you put your energy and attention is
where you get results.**

What you focus your thinking on with great consistency over time becomes the reality you will experience. This is the secret to effectively using your mental "magic wand".

Learning to intentionally direct the flow of your thoughts is an essential skill in creating a deliberate life. Mastering your mind is very much like learning how to hold your breath for a long time. When you first start deliberately focusing your attention on the things you desire, you might find that you can only do it for a short period of time until the old thought patterns start to creep in.

For example, let's say that you are retraining your thinking to focus on creating making money doing work you feel passionate about. As you think about your new business and how cool it would be to make a living doing work you love, your thought processes might look like this:

"Wow...I only need ten clients per week to make what I'm making now in my other job. That's seems pretty do-able..."

"It won't take too much marketing. And once I get a few clients, I'm sure they will refer new clients..."

"I wonder if people will really want the services I'm providing… maybe this community isn't ready for me yet…"

"You know, when I talk about my work, no one really seems to get what I do…how am I going to market myself…and if I can't explain what I do…how will I get clients….how will I make money….I've tried to make these kinds of changes in my life before and everyone just laughed at me…and I went broke…and ended up having to get another job…"

"Nothing I ever do like this has worked out before…"

"This will never work. I'm nuts for even thinking this could be possible for me…"

Your beginning thoughts are the first key steps to building new neuropathways of successful thinking patterns. Your ending thoughts are just your old neuropathways kicking in and taking over.

It's easy when your thoughts keep ending up with the default thinking process to give up and quit trying to make a change. It's to be expected that you may even feel frustrated with your thinking. You KNOW you want to make a change but you seem to be "stuck".

You're not stuck. You have old programming that needs to be rewritten.

Think about this. Where you put your energy and attention is where you get results. If you are thinking about how "stuck" you are and how, no matter how hard you try, you just can't seem to hold your positive thoughts for very long, where is your energy and attention?

On your feeling "stuck", right?

And if you are focusing on feeling "stuck", according to the Law of Focused Success, you will only create more experiences that are in alignment with feeling "stuck".

Your mind is so powerful and changing it really does require discipline, attention and, most importantly...time.

In order to speed up your process of building a new mindset, pay attention and focus on the few minutes that you successfully focused your thinking in the direction that you want it to go. If you mentally berate yourself for not "getting it right", you're only putting your focus on what you don't want.

In order to direct the flow of your thinking and creating most effectively, you have to focus on everything you want, even the kind of thinking you want.

When you focus on and acknowledge your successes (however small they might seem), then your successes, by Law of Focused Success, will grow.

The more experience and practice you have with shifting your focus in the direction you choose, the easier it gets and the longer you can do it. And, most importantly, as you take these new baby steps in your thinking, you lay down the first building blocks of your new neuropathways.

Every thought in the right direction is important and leads to bigger and better thinking and intentional and deliberate creating.

Exercises:

1. Write a story about something that you really want to experience in your life. Really get into the details. Writing is a powerful way to focus your thought processes. While you are

putting your thoughts to paper, you are focusing your thinking in a strong way that helps you maintain your thought form for a long time.

2. As you wake up in the morning, practice thinking thoughts about what you want to experience in your life. Your sleepy mind is open to new ideas and thoughts and your imagination is still zooming as you are waking. Really let yourself go wild!

The thoughts you start your day with carry a vibration that can set the tone and mood for your day. Good days and focusing on celebrating good days, create more good days!

Karen Curry

The disciples said to Jesus, "Tell us what the Kingdom of Heaven is like." He said to them, "It is like a mustard seed, the smallest of all seeds. But when it falls on tilled soil, it produces a great plant and becomes a shelter for the birds of the sky."

-**Thomas**

Chapter Six

You are Fully Open to The Magic of the Universe Helping You With Every Step of Creation. Miracles Happen to You Every Day.

Focused Review:

Your thoughts and feelings create a vibration. Your vibration determines the experiences you "attract" into your life.

You are naturally abundant. Abundance is your natural vibration. Your creative powers work easily and effortlessly all the time. It is your job to direct them.

You are supported on your Earth Journey by specialized Loving Forces who guide you and give you information to keep you focused on the maximum expression of your soul.

Where you put your energy and attention is where you get growth in your life.

We dance delicately on this Earth, gently balancing perception of our humanity and Divinity. For thousands of years prophets and ancient cultures have spoken and written of the coming of a New Earth, the true advent of an intentional "Heaven on Earth".

We cannot create "Heaven on Earth" until we shatter the paradigm of an external Heaven and God. The minute we perceive our Divinity as being outside of ourselves and Heaven as being someplace far away, we deny ourselves the power and purpose of our existence here on Earth.

God is always growing. And, as Holograms of the Divine, we are also always growing. Growth and expansion is the natural order of all life everywhere. Life without growth and expansion is death.

Our job as cells in the God-Body is to anchor the energy of the Divine in the density of the third dimension. God vibrates at a very high speed, probably beyond the speed of light. It is easy for God, and us as Holograms of the Divine, to exist at a high vibrational state.

We are Light Beings. We naturally work at the speed of light and thought.

Growth and expansion of the Divine is about experiencing Divinity in physical form in the third dimension. Earth is one of the magnificent places in the Universe where that is possible. Manifesting as a human gives us the exquisite job of living God in form in the third dimension.

Many spiritual teachers on the planet right now talk about the evolution of Earth and the process of ascension. Although we are here to raise our vibrational frequency, the purpose of ascension is not to leave our bodies and transcend the Earth experience. That's just escaping the Earth realm. You get to do that when you choose to die and leave your physical form.

The trick to really living and creating a true Heaven on Earth is to *descend* instead of ascend. Get here. Be here. Live your Heavenly Nature in form in the third dimension.

> *"There are two ways to live: you can live as if nothing is a*
> *miracle; you can live as if everything is a miracle."*
>
> -Albert Einstein

One of the most difficult, but necessary, spiritual skills is "surrendering" to the God Within. This is one of the most misunderstood spiritual ideas and yet, it is crucial that we learn how to surrender if we are to create a true Heavenly Earth.

Surrendering is not martyrdom. Surrendering is not doing things you don't want to do because "spirit" told you to do it. Surrendering is not suffering, compromising or taking leaps of "faith" when you are frustrated with waiting and then being tortured by the consequences.

Surrendering is allowing the God in you to line up your vibration with the reality you choose to perceive yourself in. Surrendering is "acting as if" you are already living what you want to be living.

Abundance teachings tell us to "act as if" we are already experiencing the abundance we are seeking. Act as if you are already rich. Act as if you have the car you desire, the house you dream of and all the things you want.

What does it mean to "act as if"?

I have watched many people "act as if" they have the money they want, go out and actually spend their real money on goods and services, and then wonder the next day why their bank account balance is so low. That's not "acting as if." That's going out of order and is usually rooted in frustration and desperation. You are "acting as if" because you are sick of waiting or you're scared.

"Acting as if" does not mean taking action "as if" were true before all the supporting resources have manifested. You can, however, use your imagination and pretend. Pretending is one of the most powerful creative energies available to humans.

I have a friend who wanted to travel around the world. Every Sunday for more than a year, she would pack her suitcase as if she was leaving for her globe-trotting journey, stand in line at the ticket counter at the airport, pretend she was checking in and then enjoy the energy of the ambiance of the airport. She did eventually go on that trip.

She was "acting as if" she was taking her dream journey. But she didn't buy the ticket and go until all the pieces were in order. It is a third dimensional world.

Things have to happen in linear order on Earth. It's the nature of the third dimension. We experience time and distance here. When we try to jump out of order we simply create chaos, especially when we haven't completely rewired our physiology.

Once you really master your Divine Power and you live out your full creative potential, it is possible to take great leaps of faith. But, if you do not completely, deeply believe that something is going to happen, if you still have underlying fears or limiting beliefs about knowing that something will manifest, beyond a doubt, then do not take action.

Faith is not hope. Faith is pure and relentless knowing. It is an act of unwavering certainty and surrender.

The delicate dance between humanity and Divinity starts in the human brain. The right hemisphere receives Divine Inspiration, the left hemisphere translates it into human action. The right brain conceives the "what". The left-brain conceives the "how".

The brain is just an organ, like the heart and the liver. Its function is to think, translate data and regulate the nervous system. Your heart doesn't have the option to do anything other than beat. Your brain doesn't have the option to do anything other than think.

When we live in the paradigm of a separate God, we think that we have to come up with all the answers. We have to take our inspiration and figure out "how" we are going to make it happen. As you may have experienced yourself, this can put you under tremendous pressure, especially when you have an inspiration that is bigger than you know how to create.

This is where a lot of people get lost in the creative process. We think we have to come up with the "how" things will happen and we close ourselves off to the constant possibility of miracles.

Thinking is to the brain as beating is to the heart. But the human brain presents challenges to us that the physical heart does not. In the brain we experience not only thinking, but also consciousness. Our Divine Awareness is perceived with the brain and we are given the task of sorting out Divine Thought and human thought, both of which are crucial on the Earthly plane.

Our human thoughts are vital. We need human thoughts to drive a car, put on our shoes, cook and build houses. Our human thoughts are the operating system for the body.

Our Divine Awareness is the antenna or the inter-dimensional interface between our expanded Self, or the Soul, and our human Self.

But, as I stated before, thinking is happening all the time. The brain has to be still for us to hear our Divine Consciousness talking. This is why a habit of daily meditation is crucial. The thinking has to be silenced in order for you to get into the habit of being able to hear your Divine Consciousness. Meditation helps you learn to sort out the different voices in your head.

Imagine this for a moment. Your brain is like a giant chamber.

Inside this chamber, you are hearing your Divine Guidance, Consciousness and Inspiration. You are also simultaneously experiencing your old thought patterns, limiting beliefs and subconscious fears. At the same time, your thinking mind is translating all of this activity into possible actions, thinking thoughts about what you saw on TV last night, remembering an old experience and wondering what's for dinner tonight.

No wonder so many of us feel paralyzed, confused or overwhelmed.

You have to think of your brain as a muscle. In order to build muscles, you have to gently train them to make them bigger. When you first start to go to the gym, you start with small weights and gradually, over time, build up your muscle strength and mass. It takes time and repetition.

Even though the brain isn't technically a muscle, it operates the same way. You have to really build your mental "muscle" over time. You have to train it to be still, be deliberate, and hold a thought for a prolonged period of time and to know the difference between God-Mind and human mind.

It takes years for a body builder to build up his muscle mass. The process of training your brain won't necessarily take years but it is a process that has to occur over time. Remember, as you are training your brain, you are also physically changing the nature of your body. You aren't growing muscles, but you are growing neuropathways.

There is a simple strategy to learning how to use your brain to anchor the high vibration of Divine Thinking and turn it into inspired action.

Step One: Daily Meditation

It is crucial that you adopt some kind of daily meditative practice. There are a lot of techniques out there. I suggest that you experiment until you find one that works for you.

The most important part of meditating is learning to get your mind quiet enough to be able to hear Divine Mind speaking to you. You probably will never be able to fully shut off your thinking mind, just as you may never get your heart to stop beating for a while.

Regardless of what technique you use, enter into your meditative practice with intention. I suggest that you write down an intention statement each morning before you meditate to help you line your energy up with the experience that you would like to have.

Your intention might say something like this:
I intend to use this special, quiet time to connect deeply with Divine Mind and to hear clearly and understand perfectly. I intend to sit in silence and deeply integrate my understanding of my Inner Divinity and to act in accordance with my Divine Wisdom each moment of this day.

Step Two: Clarifying and expressing your desires
God whispers within us through desire. God wants what you want. The blueprint for the Divine is within you and communicated through you with hopes, wishes and dreams. These are the direction points given to us by our Divinity Within.

When you turn away from your dreams and desires, you are turning away from your Inner Divinity and shutting off your access to unlimited re-Sources and miracles.

You have to have dreams and desires. These are the catalysts that inspire growth and expansion.

Step Three: Know that your desires will manifest into form
Faith is the unwavering knowingness that your desires will

manifest as part of your reality. The knowingness carries a certain vibration that lines up your consciousness with the reality you choose to experience.

You will allow yourself to experience a desire to the degree to which you believe it is a possibility for you.

When you can exist in a state of certainty and knowingness, then you can allow the natural flow of miracles to enter into your life and then take action accordingly.

Step Four: Take actions that are in alignment with your desires and beliefs

"Act as if" your desires are coming true. And make sure that your actions are leading up to what you want. I see so many people waiting for "miracles" who forget that creation in this dimension is a co-creative process. You can't just sit back in your cave and wait for the situation to magically show up. You have to do your part.

If you're going to be a best-selling author, then you better be spending time working on writing your best-selling book, or hire a ghostwriter. If you are planning on having a lot of money, then you better have a real plan on how you are going to save and invest your money when it shows up.

You have to take earthly actions that line up the frequency of what you expect in the third dimension. If you are not making the necessary preparations to receive your miracle, then you may want to re-evaluate whether you really want what you want or believe that it can really happen for you.

Miracles are wonderful works done by the Power of God. If the Power of God resides within us and our vehicle for this power is our human form, then we as humans have to co-facilitate our miracles by getting ready for their manifestation and surrendering to the process of creation.

This is the supreme expression of the spiritual concept of "surrender". The human mind that is co-creating with Divine Mind operates like a beautiful machine. Inspiration comes in. Desire is triggered. Imagination and emotion take over with delight and the human mind begins to imagine the possibilities.

The envisioning of the earthly possibilities is the translation of Divine Inspiration into human form. Once the possibilities are envisioned then you begin to prepare the way. "Act as if" your vision is coming into form.

And then you surrender. You wait until the circumstances in your outer reality show up to give you the next steps to follow for creation. Our human experience is a metaphorical experience of the Divine. Our outer world is God's world. Miracles show up daily, even hourly, in our outer reality, if we expect them.

We get inspired with big ideas, often times ideas that we don't know how to "do." Let's say, for example, that you wanted to be a best-selling author, but you didn't know how to make that happen.

First you begin the process by taking the inspiration and turning it into inspired action. You write a book.

Over time as you are writing your book, you feel and imagine yourself as a best-selling author. Maybe you even pretend a little bit and you create a fake New York Times Best Seller list that you tape on your office wall.

As you are working on your book, you realize that you keep meeting people who are authors and publishers. (Funny how you never noticed this before!) One evening you are at a dinner party at a friend's house and her brother is visiting from out of town. Turns out he is a publisher and has worked with several best-selling authors. The two of you have a lovely conversation and the next morning he emails you and asks you to send him your manuscript.

You send him the manuscript. He's impressed and wants to see more and before you know it, you have a publisher, your finished book is in hand, you are on a whirlwind book tour and your book is steadily climbing the best-seller list, just like you desired!

In this story there is a gentle relaxation or surrender that happens when you take action and wait with certainty and expectation. Of course, this is only one possible scenario. The cool part about co-creating with Divine Mind is that Divine Mind is waaaaaaay bigger than your human mind.

Although your left-brain is very good at figuring out possible "how" scenarios, Divine Mind truly understands the magic of unlimited possibility. Surrendering is letting go of pre-conceived ideas about "how" your inspiration will manifest. You simply need only to know that it will manifest and all you have to do is get ready for it and pay attention to the evidence in your outer reality.

This process of knowing and surrendering creates a vibration that is in alignment with what it is that you want to experience. The more you hold this vibration by staying in a place of certainty with your expectation, the faster your vibration aligns with the unlimited possibilities that will help you perceive your desire into form.

The marriage between the Power of God within you and your human form creates the unlimited possibility of miracles in every day life. When you let your Divine Power work its magic, you are an essential player in creating Heaven on Earth and you fulfill your Divine Role of anchoring the vibration of God deeper and deeper into the third dimension.

When you master this process, you open yourself up to experiencing the magic of the Universe and your Divine Power. Miracles will happen to you every day!

Jesus said, "Recognize what is in your sight, and that which is hidden from you will become plain to you. For there is nothing hidden which will not become manifest."

-Thomas

Chapter Seven

You are Deeply Grateful for All of Your Life Experiences. You Know They are Helping You Expand Your Thinking and Your Consciousness

----

Focused Review:

Your thoughts and feelings create a vibration. Your vibration determines the experiences you "attract" into your life.

You are naturally abundant. Abundance is your natural vibration. Your creative powers work easily and effortlessly all the time. It is your job to direct them.

You are supported on your Earth Journey by specialized Loving Forces who guide you and give you information to keep you focused on the maximum expression of your soul.

Where you put your energy and attention is where you get growth in your life.

When you relax and trust the Creation Process, everything comes to you. It's a natural and daily process.

Gratitude is defined as:

"A feeling of thankful appreciation for favors or benefits received; thankfulness"

Almost all the definitions of gratitude have the same quality of expressing thanks for things received or for blessings. Gratitude implies being thankful for something "good".

Sometimes we are faced with situations that seem truly terrible and we struggle to find the "good" in the situation. It's hard to imagine feeling grateful for an icky boss, financial worries or even the loss or illness of a child.

When you look for the "good" in a situation it implies that there is good and bad and you have to sort through the "bad" to find the "good".

What if it is all good? We are pieces of Divinity growing inside a perfect God, existing in Divine Order.

It really is all good. The challenge is in knowing how to find the "goodness".

Remember, we are infinitely wise beings.

When we choose to incarnate as people on this planet, most of us perceive only a portion of our soul essence in our incarnated form. But, even though we perceive ourselves to be "only human", we are expanded Beings of Light, here on this planet to serve God by being on the leading edge of consciousness.

What does that mean?

You are a large, wise being whose job it is to serve God by thinking, desiring and creating. As you think, desire and create, you are helping God. Everything in your life, you created to help yourself, and consequently God, grow and evolve. Your Bigger You, your Higher Self, as we sometimes call it, is working with your human self to help you create experiences that further your growth and consciousness expansion. Your Higher Self is always "talking" to you, using the Language of Emotions.

Learning to use your Mind and listen to your emotions (The language of your Higher Self) to create a life you truly desire is a skill that can help you radically create experiences that are in alignment with what you truly desire. Your focus, deliberate thoughts and intentions allow you to co-create your reality with your Higher Self, instead of feeling like a hapless victim of your reality.

So, think about this for a minute. If your life is being directed and co-created by Big You and Human You with the purpose of helping you grow and expand, every situation you are creating is, by nature "good", because it is helping you grow.

It is very easy to question the "wisdom" of your Higher Self who is working with you to further your evolution. I mean, why would you intentionally create painful situations, health challenges, financial struggles, etc.? It's easy to wonder if your Higher Self has lost its mind!

The secret to understanding the infinite wisdom of the Higher Self is to stop placing a value judgment on an experience or circumstance. If we can stop thinking of things as "good" or "bad", it makes it easier for us to find the lesson and the importance of the experience.

In spite of the chaos that we sometimes feel, we really live in a balanced, ordered Universe. The Chinese Daoists explain it with the concept of Yin and Yang. In the West we sometimes refer to it as masculine and feminine.

Western thinking about the concept of balance is pretty clear.

If you were to draw a Western version of the Yin/Yang symbol it might look like a circle, sliced precisely in half, one half white, one half black:

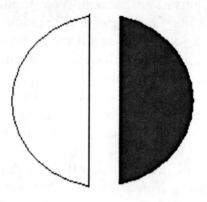

But the Eastern version looks like this:

Notice how in the Eastern version, there is no clear line and there is Yin within the Yang and Yang within the Yin. Balance in the East is really not all Yin or all Yang. All is contained within the whole.

Balance is more about cycles and flow, not an equal measurement of two polar opposites. The seeds of spring still exist deep in the ground resting during the darkness of winter, Yang waiting within Yin for its turn. The heat of summer can quickly be cooled by a rainstorm, Yin impacting Yang.

Prosperity teachers will tell you that you have to create space in order to bring in something new. You won't attract more things into your life if you don't know where to put them. You won't attract more money than you can handle if you don't have a money management plan. You can't attract a new relationship if you are still stuck in an old one (even if you are emotionally stuck.)

In Prosperity Boot Camp, one of the teleseminars I teach, sometimes my fastest, most successful students often experience cataclysmic "openings" in their lives. Friends vibrate away. They suddenly get laid off from jobs they hated. Change happens quickly in response to their plans and clarified desires.

Change can feel uncomfortable for sure. But the greatest amount of growth in life occurs when we are just a little beyond our comfort zone. The fear comes, not so much from the thought of the fulfillment of the desire but from the unknown journey that leads to the desired end.

The bougainvillea grows more beautiful and hardy when you let it dry out a bit. Many varieties of wine grapes get bigger and sweeter when you let the plant "suffer". Many plants grow better with a little deprivation because if encourages the roots to grow deeper in search of nutrients.

For people, challenges and going beyond what is known to us, forces us to deepen our roots and to draw deeper from our Source. It forces us to re-evaluate our commitment to ourselves and to the growth of our consciousness. Remember, life is meant to be an intentional journey.

You have to get out of being stuck if you want to grow. If you are not changing and not doing something new, you are not growing. And if you are not growing, you are not living. You are dying.

There is a balance between growth and rest, birth and death, comfort and discomfort. Each contained within the other. Not 50% of one and 50% of the other. It's a cycle and one without the other is either burn-out or stagnation. Neither of which is productive.

We run into trouble when we start to judge and quantify our painful experiences, which are really your most powerful Points of Evolution. These powerful turning points are not about "suffering". Suffering connotes martyrdom and pain. Suffering is "bad".

It only feels painful and negative when you judge it or even quantify it. Discomfort is not bad, nor is it really good. It is simply a symptom of your growth and evolution. You are learning something new.

The New You, the Bigger, Imagined You is creating discomfort to bring to your awareness that you aren't stretching yourself to meet your own bigger ideas about who you are, what you could be doing or having. The discomfort is really your Soul telling you to "catch up" with your dreams.

It only becomes problematic when you evaluate it and determine that discomfort feels "bad". When it feels "bad" you either try to avoid it, or you dive deep into it and embrace it as a lifestyle without rest.

Yes, it's true. Some of us are addicted to suffering. It is the only perception we know.

Everything, even the worst situations you have faced in your life, have a balance in them. Every pain you have experienced has a blessing or a gift in it. And when you can find the gift and the blessing, then you can move into gratitude and true forgiveness. But, you have to find the balance of the entire experiential equation.

When you discover the balance, the outer circumstances will no longer keep you trapped in pain and the illusion of suffering.

You will set yourself free from being a victim of something you maybe didn't even feel that you had control over.

Try this. Think of a terrible thing that has happened to you or a challenging situation in your life right now. Now make a list of all the terrible things related to this experience.

Last year I had some moments of feeling frustrated with the rate of growth of my business.

Here is an example of my List of Pain:

I'm not well known enough.
I haven't written or published enough.
A mentor or benefactor hasn't noticed me.
I haven't had the money to market myself.
I haven't had the time I need to build my business.
I don't have enough clients.
I don't have the money to create products and professional looking materials.
I've had kids and they keep me really busy.
I haven't had clarity to grow my business.
I didn't think my message would sell.

For each one of those reasons I felt stuck in my business, there was a pay-off or secondary gain.

Recognizing the pay-off for the pain helps you move into gratitude for the situation. Each pay-off is in direct response to each pain listed.

Here is my Pay-off list:

I don't owe anyone anything. I have high self-esteem and I am self-reliant.
I have been deeply motivated to learn more about marketing and self-promotion.
I have learned about my self-worth and value.
I have had to work up from the bottom and it makes me a good role model.
I am always inspired to learn about publishing and writing.
My challenges have taught me to create low-cost websites and digital products.
I have learned how to manage work, time, self-care and family.
My kids have become inspired to help me.
I have learned from my kids.
My challenges have made me get clarity and experiment.
I have moved way beyond my comfort zone, and grown.
I have matured and grown my message.

When I moved out of fear, frustration and feeling overwhelmed about my business, then I could see where my struggles had helped me grow, both personally and professionally. When I completed this list, I felt so grateful for my challenges and I could see the balanced plan of growth that was available to me.

There was no pain without a pay-off. My experience was not "bad". It was balanced. You can do this process on any situation or person in your life. It is a crucial process if you desire to make change.

Remember the Law of Focused Success: Where you put your energy and attention is where you get results.

If you are focusing on a situation that is painful, frustrating or keeping you in a place where you feel stuck and you are deeply focused on these feelings, what are you creating more of?

Your focus will determine what you create. Moving out of the pain and into the gratitude gives you the momentum to create what you want from the situation.

You can't change a situation you hate.

When you focus on the gratitude and the growth that is occurring in your life, you create more things to be grateful for and more growth.

And it won't feel "bad".

After you have written your pain and pay-off list, write yourself, or the person who is challenging you, a thank you note for helping you create a situation that helped you grow.

Take a deep breath when you are done and just enjoy the feeling of release. You have found the purpose behind the pain and now you are free to create and grow.

The more you do this process on every challenging aspect of your life, the more you set yourself free from old stories and past traumas that may have been keeping you from really living and growing.

Remember, it's all good!

Remember The Law of Focused Success:

"Where You Put Your Energy And Attention Is Where You Get Growth"

When you embrace all of life's experiences and focus on the intention of growth and expansion, by the Law of Focused Success, you get more growth and expansion.

When you resist the experience and spend your time and energy on hating all the aspects of your life circumstances, unconsciously, you are growing more resistance and experiencing more aspects of the "problem" that you hate.

Now think about this for a moment. Emotions are simply different vibrational levels. Joyful emotions are faster and therefore lighter and more expansive by nature. Sadness, anger and grief are slower vibrations and are felt as being dense and heavy.

When we are feeling joyful, we vibrate so quickly and expansively that we want to "dance for joy" and we feel light on our feet.

When we feel sad, we feel "heavy" with sorrow and our energy goes away.

Joy causes an expansion (growth) of our Essence and sadness manifests as a contraction (decrease) of our Essence.

If the purpose of life is growth and expansion (our service to God), then our goal is to move more closely to the fullest expression of our joy. That takes a little attitudinal adjustment sometimes!

I want to make one important point here. One of the things I see happening in the "New Thought" or "New Age" consciousness movement is this strong focus on positive thinking and happy thoughts. What I have witnessed and even sometimes have felt myself is the belief that it is not "okay" to feel bad or sad or even to struggle.

Working towards the fullest expression of joy is our goal; please note that I am not in any way suggesting that this is not true. But, we are where we are. And, like it or not, life will do what it does and sometimes we get curve balls like unexpected illnesses, tragedies and even deaths we didn't anticipate.

Sometimes you will feel frustrated, angry, stuck or despairing. If it's all good, then feeling "bad" is also all totally okay. It is all too easy to get into a terrible emotional rut when you feel bad and walk around focusing on your "stuckness" and just create more sadness, anger, frustration, etc.

Remember, where you put your energy and attention is where you get results. If you are resisting where you are at the moment, you will really struggle with moving towards joyful expression. Allow yourself to feel what you feel. Recognize that those feelings are telling you that you want something different than what you are experiencing and allow yourself to begin to think about what you would like to be experiencing instead.

Our "bad" feelings are simply our Higher Self communicating with us and helping us clarify what we really want.

If you are in a situation you hate, it is important to identify the fact that you don't feel good in the situation. Noticing that you are feeling dense feelings will allow yourself to get really clear about what you don't want to be experiencing and also, hopefully, start getting more clarity about what you do want to be experiencing.

Just shifting your focus toward what you do want will begin the process of moving yourself closer to your growth and expansion and consequently, you will begin to feel better.

It is hard to change a situation you hate. When you hate your conditions, you are focusing on all the things you don't like and don't want. According to the Law of Focused Success, the only thing you are growing when you are focusing on how "bad" things are and how much you hate them, is more "bad" and hateful experiences.

And you know you don't want more of that, right?

So, if you are in the middle of a situation you hate, the key to catapulting yourself out of it and into a different reality and experience is to begin to appreciate the conditions you are in.

When you are focusing on all the things you appreciate about your circumstances, you are putting your attention and energy into growing more opportunities to experience that which you appreciate, instead of icky stuff you hate.

So how does this look in real life?

Let's say you are in the middle of transitioning out of a job you hate. Maybe you inherited this business from your father when he passed away and you felt obligated to carry on.

You have informed your employees and clients that you are closing the business and several of your key employees have left. Your clients are freaking out and pressuring you to close out their contracts because they are afraid you will bail on them, even though you intend to honor your commitments.

You are overworked, tired, frustrated and hate the situation you are in. But, you feel strongly that you have to honor your agreements and fulfill your contracts as part of closing your business.

If you are resisting the process and focusing on all the aspects of the situation you hate, you will only create more tension, stress and unpleasantness for yourself and maybe even for the few employees who are still hanging out with you.

When you go home, you might feel over-stimulated and grouchy and you snap at your kids and your partner, who in turn react by treating you in ways that don't feel supportive.

You stop taking care of your body (too busy), smoke a lot (stress), sleep fitfully (more stress) and the situation just gets more and more intense as you grow in your hatred of the situation.

You can see how difficult it is to change the experience of the situation when the focus is on what you don't want. And, by the Law of Focused Success you might even create more struggle, stress and hardship by really directing energy and attention to all the things you really hate about your circumstances.

Imagine how different your experience might be if your focus was here instead:

"How great that I have had this wonderful employment that has created the financial resources that helped me buy a nice home and provide for my children."

"As I pay these bills, I am so grateful to have been served by all of these wonderful vendors who have helped me grow my business."

"What wonderful employees I have. They have stayed with me even through the darkest moments of my business."

"I really appreciate my clients. They have given me years of opportunities to share my wisdom and knowledge. I truly appreciate their deep commitment to detail and how they always ask me for more information to make sure that our project works beautifully as it serves others."

"What a great desk chair! It has molded itself to my body and holds me up so comfortably..."

"I really appreciate my Higher Self. It has created a wonderful opportunity for me to grow and expand my experience here in this life. I am so clever to create this growth for myself!"

Can you see how, when your focus is on all things that are working and finding aspects of appreciation, even in the things that seem challenging, your focus is on creating more experiences that you appreciate?

If you are in a situation you hate, and struggling to find your way out, shift your focus on all the things you appreciate about the situation. It isn't until you fall in love with your situation that you will see real change. Be grateful for the clarity and the lessons you are giving yourself. The more you focus on what you appreciate and love about your situation, the more you will create opportunities for yourself to experience more and more joy, growth and expansion.

Exercises:

1. Think about a challenging situation you are facing right now. Make a list of all the things you don't like about the situation. When you are done, go back through your list and find the hidden benefits of the things you hate about the situation. Write a letter of appreciation to the person or situation that is giving you so much challenge.

2. If you are working on creating a new condition in your life, find evidence that circumstances of your new situation are already in your life right now.

For example, if you are intending to attract your soul mate, where in your life right now are you already experiencing great love, joy and commitment? Write down your gratitude.

3. When you are having an experience that you don't like, catch your thoughts and immediately ask yourself what would you like to be experiencing instead? Express your gratitude for the clarity.

Inside the Body of God

Jesus said to them, "When you make the two one, and when you make the inside like the outside and the outside like the inside; then you will enter the Kingdom."

-Thomas

Inside the Body of God

Chapter Eight

Your Positive Emotions Show You that Your Attention is in Alignment with Your Desires. You Are on Your Way to Creating Exactly What You Want.

Focused Review:

Your thoughts and feelings create a vibration. Your vibration determines the experiences you "attract" into your life.

You are naturally abundant. Abundance is your natural vibration. Your creative powers work easily and effortlessly all the time. It is your job to direct them.

You are supported on your Earth Journey by specialized Loving Forces who guide you and give you information to keep you focused on the maximum expression of your soul.

Where you put your energy and attention is where you get growth in your life.

When you relax and trust the Creation Process, everything comes to you. It's a natural and daily process.

Gratitude and appreciation are a powerful creative vibration that helps you focus on what you want with delight.

You are an infinite being with access to all the information you need. But, you're also experiencing being human. And the density of the third-dimensional experience can be perceived as confusing and disorienting.

When we study the cells of the body, science has discovered that there are numerous encoded messages within a cell and the structure of the cell to help it know its role and keep its environment balanced to ensure optimal function.

As cells in the Body of God, we also have numerous systems to guide us and help us remember why we incarnated, keep us balanced and ensure our optimal function.

Your emotional system is one of the most powerful navigation tools you have. Your emotions are like your own personal inner compass. You can never NOT know what to do or which direction to go. Never.

But, sometimes we don't always know how to interpret the information we are sending ourselves. Or we might not like the answer we receive.

One of the greatest gifts that we have as humans is our ability to control our experiences and all of the resources and tools available to us. We can choose to hear our Inner Wisdom and intuition, open up our perception to Unseen Loving Forces and use our emotions to guide us along the path.

But, we can also, just as easily, allow ourselves to be conditioned to forget that we have all of these powerful resources available to us.

The bottom line is this. You can always know what to do and where to go with your life. The information you seek is always available to you. You just have to remember how to use it for your highest good.

We are "hard-wired" to be happy. Ancient Chinese medicine is based on the concept that we have energetic circuits called meridians. When we are happy and healthy, life force energy, called chi, flows without interruption in a positive direction throughout our body and energy field.

Anytime we experience a trauma, a painful emotional event or some kind of injury, the flow of our life force energy gets blocked or disrupted. Acupuncture, which is the placement of tiny needles on key energy meridian intersection points helps unblock the energy disruptions and restores the flow of chi to its abundant, positive direction.

Over the past 15 years, we have seen tremendous evolution in the field of Energy Psychology. Energy Psychologists have studied the effects of emotions on the body and the energy system and determined that emotional trauma impacts the body and the energy field just as powerfully as physical trauma.

The field of Energy Psychology has taught us that acupuncture and acupressure techniques, such as the Emotional Freedom Techniques (EFT) can help "heal" emotional trauma and restore the body back to its natural energetic state of happiness and abundance.

When we are happy, our life force energy runs through our bodies and energy fields in a positive direction. Emotions can cause disruptions in our energy field and, if we don't know how to understand and process emotions, these disruptions can ultimately lead to blocks in our Life Force Energy.

Anytime Life Force Energy is blocked, you will experience physical symptoms and even illness. Being "stuck" in negative emotional patterns not only takes you away from your natural abundant and happy state, it can actually contribute to the breakdown of your physical body.

When you vibrate and energetically line up with perceptions that are in alignment with your vibration, you are sending out waves of energy. Remember, vibrations travel in a wave-like fashion.

Happiness is the base-line frequency of your vibrational wave when you are feeling abundant and prosperous. A base-line frequency of happiness is natural, normal and healthy.

The happier you feel, the faster your vibration and the more you attract experiences that reflect your happiness. The faster your vibration, the less time you spend experiencing the normal peaks and troughs that come with a vibrational wave. Your wave is faster and the peaks and troughs are shorter in height and duration.

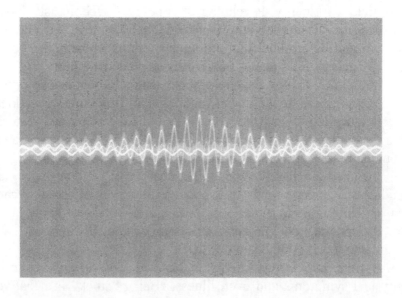

This is why when you feel good, it seems like you are not experiencing as much sadness or even extreme bliss. There is an even balance between the undulations of the wave and you barely notice the subtle shifts in your vibration.

When your vibration is low, you lower your base-line frequency from happiness to depression or frustration, the wave travels slower and the peaks and troughs are higher, more pronounced and last longer. When you slow your vibration down, it gets easier to align with chaos and to feel stuck in energies and situations that don't seem to change very easily.

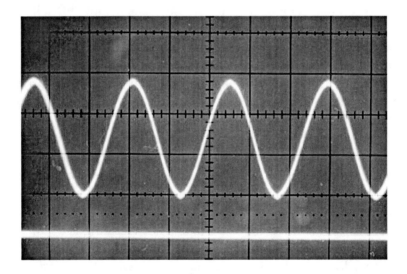

Raising your frequency requires deliberate thinking and disciplined attention to your emotional state. It's a simple process but not always easy because it can take time to make a lasting shift. Remember, when you make the decision to make this change, you are often rewiring a lifetime of biology.

You can control your emotional state and the vibrational frequency you radiate. The trick is learning how to deliberately control your vibrational state and, at the same time, letting your emotional energy flow and communicate to you the way it is intended.

Remember, your natural state is abundance. Your body is "hard-wired" to be abundant. But, you are simultaneously vibrating and experiencing undulations on your emotional wave. You will vibrate faster when you focus on your abundance, success and experiences you want to have.

Your vibration slows down when you think about your perceived blocks, pains and limitations. These thoughts take you away from your abundant vibration.

You will ALWAYS have experiences that may seem "bad". You NEED to have experiences that don't always feel great. Your seemingly bad experiences give you clarity to help you deepen your awareness of what you do want in order for you to expand and grow.

Think about this. What if you were always happy...no undulations on your emotional wave...just happy all the time. As much as we fantasize that this is the experience we choose to have, a pure happy sine wave, with no opposite experiences, does not vibrate.

And, as we know, a sine wave that is not vibrating is dead.

Life without the seemingly bad experiences is a life without the potential for growth. The challenge is allowing the emotions of the "bad" experiences to fulfill their purpose of helping us gain clarity and evolve, and to not get stuck in the negativity.

We have a tendency to judge our emotional experiences as either good or bad. Emotional energy is simply the DNA of your soul talking to you. It is neither good, nor bad. But when we label certain kinds of feelings as bad, resist them and define ourselves by our experience of them, then we run the risk of identifying with the low end of our sine wave, placing our focus here and consequently slowing the vibration down.

Try this. Say these statements slowly to yourself in the mirror:

I am sad.
I am tired.
I am depressed.
I am angry.
I am frustrated.

I am happy.
I am glad.
I am joyful.

Can you feel the difference in the energies of these statements? We are not our emotions. To say you are your emotions is the same as a screen door saying that it is the wind. You are experiencing your emotions and they are talking to you, giving you direction and helping you clarify your direction and desires.

The minute you identify with your emotions and "become" them is the minute you begin to trap yourself in a "story" that takes you away from your natural abundant state. Your emotions are supposed to flow through you, as the wind blows through a screen door. Your job is to listen to them, and use them to gain clarity and a deeper understanding of your Desires and beliefs.

Your feelings are the compass of your soul's journey. Your emotions are simply letting you know whether you want more of a situation that feels good or something different from a situation that feels bad.

Creation always starts with a Desire. Your Desires and Inspirations are God whispering your life's direction to you. As you experience your Desire, an aspect of your Unlimited Self is already living the Desire. In the third dimension, our perceptions can be limited by time and space. The expanded aspect of ourselves lives outside of the confines of the third dimension. Desires are fulfilled instantly.

So, when you have a Desire, there is a part of you that is already living it. In order to have the Desire fulfilled in the third dimension, you have to be vibrationally lined up with the experience you are wanting. Your emotions indicate to you whether your vibrations are lined up or not.

Let's say you want to move into a nicer, bigger house. As soon as you have the Desire, vibrationally there is a part of you that is already living in that house. The more you think about moving into that house, the more excited and delighted you feel. This is your internal emotional compass telling you that this excited, delighted vibration is lining you up with your Desire and you are on your way to creating exactly what you want.

According to the Law of Focused Success, where you put your energy and attention is where you get results. As you focus on how good your Desire to live in a nicer house feels, and you delightfully imagine where you will place all the furniture, how it will feel to watch the sun set on your new deck and all the parties you will have with your friends and family, your vibration goes up and begins to align with the reality of the new house.

The more you can see and feel this experience, the faster and easier it is for you to begin to have this experience in your third dimensional reality.

But, what if you have a lot of uncleared fears and limiting beliefs that keep you from feeling excited about your Desire?

Let's say that every time you start to think about living in a nicer, bigger house, you feel worried and sad because you don't think it's possible for you to actually live in a house like that. How will you ever earn the money?

According to the Law of Focused Success, if you are feeling crummy about living in a newer, bigger house, your energy and attention are focused on feeling crummy and the impossibility that you could actually have this great experience. The more you focus on the impossible as being impossible, the more impossible the experience becomes.

Your emotions are helping you see how close you are to vibrating in alignment with your Desire. The better you feel about a Desire, the closer you are to creating it and attracting it into your life.

When a Desire triggers negative emotions, your Divine Self is sending you a message and guiding you back to your Abundant Self. Your emotions, positive and negative are just messages to help you understand where you are on the map of your soul's journey. Interpret them correctly and you will become a Master Alchemist in your life.

When you are experiencing negative emotions, you are giving yourself vital information about your creative process. It is crucial to ask yourself some key questions when you are having negative feelings.

The first question to ask yourself is do you REALLY want what you are intending? We are often conditioned to ask for what we think we should want, as opposed to what we really want. Clarifying your Desire and making sure it is a pure Desire from your heart instead of your head is crucial.

Hint: A pure desire is EXCITING! A head-based desire doesn't spark a deep positive emotional response.

If you trust that your Desire is really what you want, then the next question to ask yourself is do you have any limiting beliefs that are keeping you from allowing yourself to believe that your Desire can come true for you?

If you truly believe that you can have what you desire, then you will feel good and excitedly anticipate the experience you are wanting. Your good feelings show you that your vibrations match your intentions.

If you experience bad feelings then your emotions are telling you that you have limiting beliefs and thoughts that are keeping you from vibrating in alignment with your Desire. This is a wonderful opportunity for you to push through your conditioning and grow more deeply into consciously experiencing your natural Divine Self.

Your bad feelings are simply letting you know that you have some work to do on your thinking patterns. With discipline, intention and practice you can realign your psycho-biology with your natural abundant state.

Emotions are really the karma that keeps us densely bound to the third dimension. When we are not processing emotional energy and using it as a compass, we create dense energies that trap us, and even those we love, into heavy patterns that can keep us trapped for lifetimes.

The time for healing the emotional karma of the planet is now. Emotions have to move and flow freely like the wind in order for us to really enjoy the abundance that is available to us. For lifetimes we have been stuck in emotional energy that hasn't moved. We have defined ourselves by our emotions creating histories of stories that keep us from our abundant state.

There is a dark side to "positive" thinking. When we judge emotions as "bad" or "negative" and we work hard mentally to avoid them or turn them around, we shut down our inner compass.

This can be tricky. You don't want to get stuck in an emotional experience but you also have to let it flow. Emotions are energy. They have to move.

Imagine a glass bottle full of soda. If you take the cap off, put your thumb over the top and shake it up eventually the soda will foam up and explode everywhere. You have to take your thumb off the top to let the pressure out.

Emotional energy has to go somewhere. Just like the soda, if you don't allow for its expression, it will find somewhere to go and build up energy until it explodes, usually in the form of illness, limiting beliefs or destructive life patterns.

When you resist an experience, the focus is on resistance. And of course, the more you resist something, the more the resistance grows because your energy and attention is on resistance. Focused resistance over time creates a very slow energy wave.

Emotions flow easily when we stop judging them and really see them as directional energy. There are really no "good" or "bad" emotions. Some certainly feel better than others but that's because the ones that feel bad are telling you that you are going in the wrong direction, away from what you desire.

It doesn't feel good to stick your finger in an electrical socket for a reason.

Your positive emotions are telling you that you are headed in the direction of what you want to experience. When you feel good, you are in alignment with your Desires and you are on your way to creating exactly what you want in your life!

Exercises:

1. Pay attention to how you talk to others about emotions. Do you describe yourself by your feelings? Shift your language to reflect your emotional experience.

For example:

I am feeling sad about this.
I am experiencing frustration.
I am having a super-joyful day!

2. Make a list of 10 things you really desire in your life. How do you feel about these Desires? Are they true Heart's Desires or are they head-based Desires? Do you have limiting beliefs that are keeping you from believing you can have these experiences?

Learn EFT – the Emotional Freedom Techniques: Visit joyfulmission.com and read the "EFT For Everyone" article.

Jesus said, "Love your brother like your soul."
-Thomas

Chapter Nine

You Surround Yourself with People Who Support Your Creative Process

----

Focused Review:

Your thoughts and feelings create a vibration. Your vibration determines the experiences you "attract" into your life.

You are naturally abundant. Abundance is your natural vibration.

Your creative powers work easily and effortlessly all the time. It is your job to direct them.

You are supported on your Earth Journey by specialized Loving Forces who guide you and give you information to keep you focused on the maximum expression of your soul.

Where you put your energy and attention is where you get growth in your life.

When you relax and trust the Creation Process, everything comes to you. It's a natural and daily process.

Gratitude and appreciation is a powerful, creative vibration that helps you focus on what you want with delight.

Your Good Feelings show you that you are focusing on what you really want.

"The science of the future will be based on Sympathetic Vibrations."
-Rudolph Steiner, 1913

Even though we are having an individual experience of being alive we are still deeply communal beings. We are Brothers and Sisters of the One and together, we vibrationally create the experience of our world.

Relationships can be a tricky arena within which to play out our Divinity. It is easy for our cultural conditioning, emotions, bodies, biology and our minds to get all mixed up in some pretty dynamic expressions within our Divine Family.

We need each other. Together we maintain and project the image of the world we live in. The dramas we live out together in response to our vibrations can create tremendous bliss or horrific suffering.

We are powerfully co-creating everything that happens in our relationships both personally and globally. Our relationships, as part of our outer reality, are projections of our mindset. We are responsible for creating "good" or "bad" relationships.

The challenge in relationships is to live out the love that you have for yourself and the love that you have for your Brothers and Sisters and to do it in an unlimited loving way, without compromise.

A pretty tall order!

The key to understanding relationships is remembering that the alchemical rules of creation apply to everything, even relating to your Divine Siblings.

No one comes into your world without you having attracted that person with the sole intention of helping you further the growth and evolution of your Soul. Your playmates are in your life to help you grow.

But, as with every other aspect of your life, you have the power to create the kinds of relationships that you choose to experience. Even though it seems counter-intuitive, you can dictate how others treat you and the kinds of experiences that you want to have in relationships. And it doesn't involve controlling other people. It's all up to you.

We are radiant, magnetic beings who align with realities that match our vibration. The most important challenge in creating strong, supportive and delightful relationships is learning to love yourself, first and foremost.

If you are going to experience good relationships in which you experience great love, then it has to start with you first. When you can deeply love and appreciate the magnificent, beautiful and unique piece of the Divine you are, then you will attract others who are aligned with that energy.

Part of the challenge of relationships is that we often mistakenly believe that there are other humans out there who can "complete" us or make us feel "whole". When you understand that the whole is already contained within you, you know that there is no one outside of you who can truly make your experience of life more complete.

To really create the relationships that bring you love and joy, you have to create a life you love first. Your joy, fulfillment, delight, happiness, spiritual connection, love and sense of feeling "whole", must reside in you first before relationships that manifest these qualities can be a part of your reality.

Until then, you will attract relationships that bring you lessons to help you clarify exactly where you stand in consciousness and where it is that you seek to grow. Relationships help deepen your awareness of what you truly want to be experiencing in your reality sometimes, of course, by showing you the opposite.

Each time you feel challenged in relationships, you are presenting yourself with the opportunity to know how you want to be treated, supported and nurtured. As you grow and evolve, so do your relationships. Some playmates grow along with you. Others drift away or vibrate out of your awareness.

The trick to using relationship challenge as a springboard for your growth is remembering that we are all children of the Divine. No one is victimizing you in your relationships. You are completely and totally magnificent and loveable. And so are all your Soul Brothers and Sisters. We just co-create situations that might need some integration and a return to the Light.

It's all you anyway. Each individual who manifests in your reality is simply an outer manifestation of your inner consciousness. What is inside of you that co-created this lesson with another differentiated aspect of the Whole?

In the Earth-arena, we often forget our Divine Power and hold others responsible for things that originated first in our own consciousness. In order to create harmonious relationships, we have to first realign with Source energy and embrace the perfection within our partners, our friends and us. Only then we can begin to understand the blessings of the situation.

This returning to Light is called forgiveness and is the most important act of consciousness we can perform. When we fail to forgive, we doom ourselves to repeat, by Law of Attraction, the same or similar situations again and again.

Imagine one of your Soul Sisters having the traumatic experience as a young adolescent of being abandoned by her father.   Maybe this trauma left a scar on her heart and the experience of the abandonment left her afraid to really connect with anyone because she doesn't want to feel that vulnerable and hurt again.

Now picture this same person a little older and having intimate relationships with men.   Each time she finally relaxes into the relationship, the man leaves, sometimes in very traumatic ways. With each abandonment, this beautiful woman adds to her "belief bank" that men leave her, she is "not enough" or "too much" for someone to really love and she'll never have a soul mate relationship.

Of course, the more she repeats these experiences in reality and in consciousness, the more she continues to attract partners who energetically vibrate with her "story".   These beautiful Divine Siblings experience emotional resonance and the whole cycle repeats itself tragically and often with greater intensity.

Forgiveness is a concept that often gets confusing in its application. Forgiveness is not the condoning of the actions that may have been very damaging, painful or even out of integrity. When you forgive someone, you don't have to allow hurtful behavior or tolerate being treated as less than the magnificent being you are.

Forgiving is not something that you do for someone else. You have no responsibility to your perceived transgressor. You can't make anyone feel better about a situation ... except yourself.

Forgiveness is the process of allowing the energy of an experience to flow through you so that you may use the emotions generated to help you clarify and deepen your intentions. Forgiveness is a restoration of your God-consciousness, a return to your natural state of abundance.

When you experience a challenging situation with another person, you are having an experience that is helping you get clear about what you really want. For example, let's say a spouse in a marriage has an affair.

Naturally, the other spouse might feel shocked, betrayed, hurt, angry and a myriad of other feelings. These feelings are giving this person some important information about their life such as:

1. They may want to be loved in a deep, committed way with a partner who is faithful.
2. In consciousness, they may be straying from a commitment to themselves and their own well-being and their outer reality is demonstrating that.
3. They may have even strayed in their consciousness away from their marriage commitment (even if they, themselves have not had an affair). Their own shift of focus away from their commitment might be part of the loss of commitment energy in the marriage.

Each story is unique and the couple may have their own understandings of what has transpired in the marriage. Certainly, this kind of straying creates an emotional situation that is clearly telling someone something about their life.

Obviously, there is no formula for "right" action in this situation. There are an unlimited number of actions that they may consider taking, but they won't really finish moving through the lesson of the situation until they complete the forgiveness step.

But, before forgiveness can begin, trauma must be healed. Sometimes we co-create some powerful stuff and our bodies, minds and spirits need healing before we can begin to return to the Light. If it doesn't feel right yet to forgive, it's okay. Heal first. Process. Let the emotions run their course before you jump in to forgive.

But, as soon as you start noticing that you have a "script" or a patterned way of telling the story of your betrayal, then it's time to move into the forgiveness phase. When the experience becomes a story that defines you as a "survivor", it is crucial that you let it go and complete the forgiveness step.

You are not a "survivor". You are a "thriver".

Abundance is our natural state. We are hard-wired to be happy. When we practice forgiveness, we are simply returning our focus back on our natural state of abundance. When we are abundant, we feel safe, powerful, supported, unlimited and whole.

You cannot be abundant and a victim simultaneously.

Because we are individuated aspects of a whole God. Our Soul Brothers and Sisters are a differentiated expression of the whole contained within us. When we hold unforgiveness against one of our Divine Siblings, we are really just keeping a part of ourselves from the Light.

Anything that comes into your awareness that is not abundant or has fallen into darkness is there because your consciousness drew it to your awareness. Even news articles that you read on your computer or watch on TV are aspects of your consciousness manifested in your reality.

These situations are drawn to your awareness out of your consciousness. Your Higher Self is asking you to consciously return this aspect of your awareness back to the Light.

Every day you get a chance to facilitate the return of Collective Consciousness back to Source Energy simply by reading the news and visualizing an alternative abundant expression of the world's events. When we all work together to collectively project a new perception of a limitlessly abundant world, then we will be co-creating Heaven on Earth.

Of course, it's sometimes easier to do this with the news than it is with your personal life.

Sometimes the fastest way to forgiveness is by finding the blessings in the situation. We live in a balanced Universe. There is never pain without some kind of pay-off or blessing. There is always a gift that you receive from any situation. When you shift your focus on the blessings, it moves your consciousness back to abundance and your natural Divine state.

Let's go back to the situation with the cheating spouse. Maybe the couple ended up getting divorced and it was a nasty process. Maybe the "victim" of the infidelity didn't get a lot of alimony and had to go back to work to be able to support their children.

But, what if in that process, this person discovers that she is a powerful entrepreneur and motivational speaker? Maybe she went on to write a book about the power and beauty of marriage, even in the face of betrayal. Eventually, she meets a man who loves her and only her and together they are deeply committed and have a beautiful marriage and partnership.

None of these amazing things would have happened without the original experience of pain. The painful situation was a powerful catalyst for this woman's growth and evolution.

But it's not just about finding the blessings in the situation; it's also about releasing the experience and not using it as a defining story. When you release the story, you are removing the point of attraction in your consciousness that can potentially recreate the situation again in a different way.

If you no longer allow yourself to assume the role of victim, you will not attract the experience of being a victim again. Restoring your consciousness to your Divine abundant state, allows you to attract an abundant life experience.

As we are conditioned to focus on things that are not working, it's very easy in relationships to get distracted and focus on the irritations and the problems in connecting with each other. How much attention do we put on the habits and issues that drive us nuts when we play together versus all the good things about our Divine Playmates?

The Law of Focused Success states:

"Where you put your energy and attention is where you get results."

When you are in a relationship and you focus on all the things about your friends or partners that drive you nuts, the things that drive you crazy are more consistently brought into your outer creations. Your mindset programs your system to find evidence to support your beliefs.

The more your relationships irritate and annoy you, the more you focus on the irritation and annoyance. The more we focus on how irritated and annoyed we feel, the more we create more irritation and annoyance.

It's amazing how dramatically we can shift the quality of our relationships by simply moving our focus away from what isn't working in the relationship to what IS working.

When you move into a place of deep appreciation for your companions, you program your reality to experience good things from the people around you.

Imagine that you walk into a room and your partner is sitting in a chair scowling at you because you, once again, didn't put the lid back on the sugar bowl and you left sugar crystals on the table. Your partner is thinking about how messy you are and wondering just how did he ever manage to hook up with such a sloppy soul and what if you could just be neater and more organized...

You can just feel the resentment rolling off this guy's aura.

Now imagine that you walk into the same room and your partner is thinking how amazing it is that you always seem to find the time to take care of others, how lovely you look today and isn't he lucky to be in love with such a beautiful, compassionate woman...

Can you feel how the energy has changed?

Sometimes, especially when you are seemingly experiencing deep conflict with a person, appreciation feels like a real stretch. Start small. Even you can appreciate only the fact that this person has really nice shoelaces. What you appreciate doesn't matter as much as the fact that you are engaging in the energy of appreciation.

When you shift your energetic focus, you begin to attract a different experience with the same person. The person isn't really changing. You are changing your point of attraction when you focus on what works and what you appreciate. Your energy and attention is placed on what you DO like, what IS working and worthy of appreciation. The more you focus there, the greater the growth.

But, sometimes, regardless of the appreciation, we move out of resonance with each other.

Vibrations relate to each other. Different vibrations will modulate and influence each other. That's why someone vibrating with a high vibration can lift you up or someone who is vibrating low can bring you down.

If you have two pianos in a room and you pluck the string on one piano, the same string on the opposite piano will vibrate sympathetically. The two strings have resonance and consequently vibrate together sympathetically

Notice that the two strings, which have the same resonance, vibrate together and sympathetically. Sometimes in relationships, the difference in intention and vibration is so significant that there is no resonance and it becomes difficult to vibrate together.

When this happens, by Law of Attraction, there is no attraction. There can be love and appreciation but no vibrational alignment for certain kinds of relating. Friends and lovers sometimes simply vibrate away to different realities.

Sometimes when we have differing resonance in partnerships, we have to take actions to make room for new relationships that are more in alignment with our new vibrational state. It is very common, once you begin reclaiming your Divine Power, to find that you have outgrown some of your partnerships.

You may find that you need to take deliberate actions to change your relationships. Like a monkey with nuts in his hand, trying to reach into a narrow opening of a jar to grab more nuts, but who has to drop what he has to get more of something new, you sometimes have to empty aspects of you current life to make room for something different and better for you.

If you stay in a place of abundant thinking and appreciation, you'll see that these dynamic changes in partnerships aren't personal. It's not like you or your Divine Playmates did something wrong. It's simply that the vibrational alignment for co-creating your intention isn't there. Maybe you have different intentions and desires. In order to each experience the fulfillment of your respective desires, you may need to create in different arenas.

We are very conditioned to create perceived problems when we move out of vibrational alignment. Naturally, there is a certain discordant energy that can happen when there is a vibrational mismatch. But, if you continue to stay in a place of appreciation and loving what is good about the situation, it is possible to "vibrate apart" without tension, blaming, anger and other difficult emotions.

Of course, difficult emotions, even sadness, can be a part of this process. Allow yourself to experience your emotions and let your feelings talk to you so that you can stay very clear about what you truly desire and how you want to experience your relationship. Be clear that your intention is to change the nature of your relationship with love.

Part of being clear in relationships is knowing the kinds of experiences that you would like to have with your Soul Partners. The more clarity you have about your relationships, the easier it is to create those kinds of experiences.

When we are in resonance with each other, frequencies do modulate and affect each other; it is crucial that you intend relationships that support your creative process. When you are creating with a group of people who support your new ways of thinking and understand the power of your creative force, it helps you keep your vibrations high and focused on what you want.

In the face of the conditioning field, it sure makes things easier if you can get by with a little help from your friends! There is enormous power in deliberately creating with a group of people. The more people come together with the intention of co-creation, the more powerful the result.

In 1983, a group of Transcendental Meditators came together in co-creation with the intention to deliberately improve the quality of life in Jerusalem through prayer and meditation. Quality of life was defined by a statistical analysis of the number of fires, traffic accidents, criminal acts, stock market results and the emotional outlook of the population of the city.

Two hundred thirty four participants in this group came together each day to meditate and pray in strategic locations in the city of Jerusalem. As a result of the co-creative intention of this group, crimes, fires and accidents were reduced. In addition, it was proven that there was a high correlation between the number of people meditating and praying and the quality of life in Jerusalem. (Orme-Johnson, et. al, "International Peace Project in the Middle East," 781)

We are created in the image of the Divine. Our outer reality is merely a reflection of our relationship with our abundance consciousness. If we intend to create a world that anchors the energy of Heaven here on Earth, we have to enter into our relationships with a deep sense of responsibility.

What we live out in our outer reality and how we treat each other is a metaphorical representation of how we choose to show up for life and what we intend to create here. If we are intentionally creating an abundant world, then we must live abundantly, especially in our relationships.

As cells in the Body of God, the health of our world is the collective projection of our combined individual states of well-being. The way we treat each other is a metaphorical representation of the out-picturing of our world.

If we individually treat others with disrespect, blame, criticism or any other kinds of behavior that is out of alignment with our Divinity...if we continue to see our Soul Brothers and Sisters as anything less than the magnificent Divine Beings they are...then, in consciousness, we are contributing to the consciousness and manifestation of lack on this planet.

If you intend to consciously create a world where all people are well-fed, deeply loved, valued and educated in a way that supports the growth and evolution of their minds, bodies and spirits, then you must align with that vibration on a consciousness level and, of course, take actions that are in alignment with that vibration.

Even if you feel powerless to make a "big" difference in the world, how you relate to your own consciousness and your Soul Brothers and Sisters is a vital and very important way to co-create a beautiful, abundant world.

Love God. Love each other. Love yourself.

Mark 12:28
One of the teachers of the law came and heard them debating (Jesus and the Sadducees were debating in the previous verses). Noticing that Jesus had given them a good answer, he asked him, "Of all the commandments, which is the most important?"

"The most important one," answered Jesus, is this: 'Hear O Israel, the Lord our God, the Lord is one. Love the Lord your God with all your heart and with all your soul and with all your mind and with all your strength.' The second is this: 'Love your neighbor as yourself.' There is no commandment greater than these."

"Well said, teacher," the man replied [to Jesus]. "You are right in saying that God is one and there is no other but him. To love him with all your heart, with all your understanding, and with all your strength, and to love your neighbor as yourself is more important than all burnt offerings and sacrifices."

When Jesus saw that he had answered wisely, he said to him, "You are not far from the kingdom of God."

Exercises:

1. Write yourself a long love letter and remind yourself of your unique magnificence and the special spark of Divinity that is You, an Unlimited Child of God.

2. Answer the following question in your journal:

"Do I love my life?"

Read your response and discover what changes you may need to make to continue to create a life you truly love.

3. Make a list of any situation and person you may need to forgive. Work on forgiving one person at a time. Make a list of everything you love and appreciate about each person and a list of all the blessings you have received from having your experiences with this person.

4. Make a list of appreciation for everybody in your life. Once a week read your lists and add to them as necessary.

5. Take an inventory of all the relationships in your life. Are they uplifting and enlivening? Do you feel loved, supported and accepted for who you are? Are there things you need to say in your relationships to make them more authentic and restore them to the Light? Do you need to release some relationships that are perhaps no longer in your Highest Good?

6. Write a dream statement about your ideal friendships, partnerships and love relationships. How do you want to feel in your relationships? Are there aspects of personal self-love that

you need to expand to feel better in your relationships? Find evidence in your current relationships of your dream statement and express your gratitude.

Joyfully anticipate the creation of even more exciting, loving and fulfilling relationships.

7. Take time each day to visualize an abundant world where all people are well-fed, deeply loved, valued and educated in a way that supports the growth and evolution of their minds, bodies and spirits

Jesus said, "Whoever has something in his hand will receive more, and whoever has nothing will be deprived of even the little he has."

-Thomas

Chapter Ten

Abundant Opportunities are Always Presenting Themselves to You

----

Focused Review:

Your thoughts and feelings create a vibration. Your vibration determines the experiences you "attract" into your life.

You are naturally abundant. Abundance is your natural vibration.

Your creative powers work easily and effortlessly all the time. It is your job to direct them.

You are supported on your Earth Journey by specialized Loving Forces who guide you and give you information to keep you focused on the maximum expression of your soul.

Where you put your energy and attention is where you get growth in your life.

When you relax and trust the Creation Process, everything comes to you. It's a natural and daily process.

Gratitude and appreciation is a powerful creative vibration that helps you focus on what you want with delight.

Your Good Feelings show you that you are focusing on what you really want.

You are surrounded by Divine Siblings who seek to co-create with you. You are never alone.

"No one is kept in poverty by a shortness of supply of riches; there is more than enough for all. The visible supply is practically inexhaustible; and the invisible supply really IS inexhaustible."
- Wallace Wattles
The Science of Getting Rich

Have you ever lost your keys, spent hours looking for them and finally found them…"hiding" from you in plain sight?

What are your thoughts as you search frantically for the keys? Are you cursing yourself for losing your keys? Are you frustrated because you're going to be late because you don't have those darn keys?

Do you wonder why this "always" happens to do?

Finding your keys is a matter of focus. When your keys are lost, your focus is commonly on the lost keys. The seemingly natural thing to say to yourself is that your keys must be found.

But when you place your focus on finding the "lost" keys, your focus is on the "lost". And, by Law of Focused Success, when you are focusing on the lost keys, the keys just keep getting more lost.

Isn't is funny how when you finally give up in frustration and stop caring about the keys, or you decide to call someone and get a ride, that is the moment you usually find the keys?

And how many times were they somewhere obvious but you overlooked them again and again?

What happened that made it possible for you to see the keys

again, because you know they didn't just magically appear...?

When you shift your focus to the solution as opposed to the "lost", you can then see the keys.

You have to know that your keys can be found (easily and effortlessly) or, at the very least, give up the idea that the keys are lost, before you can have your keys as part of your life again.

Abundance is just like those keys.

Abundance is always right in front of you, sometimes "hiding in plain sight."

You just have to program your thinking to see it.

Each day we are bombarded with billions of bits of information. Imagine what your life would be like if you were aware of every single one of them—you'd probably go crazy! The clicking sound of your dog's nails on your wooden floor, the hum of the fan, the voices that surround you, airplanes flying over your house... You are saved from that sort of nerve-racking experience by a perfectly designed feature in your brain called the Reticular Activating System (RAS).

The RAS consists of a bundle of densely packed nerve cells located in the central core of the brain stem. Roughly the size of a little finger, the RAS runs from the top of the spinal cord into the middle of the brain. This area of tightly packed nerve fibers and cells contains nearly 70% of your brain's estimated 200 billion nerve cells or a total of 140 billion cells.

The RAS acts as the executive secretary for your conscious mind. It is the chief gatekeeper to screen or filter the type of data allowed to get through. Everything else is filtered out. You simply don't pay attention to those other "messages".

At any given time you are surrounded by millions of "bits" of information. The RAS is capable of processing approximately 150 "bits" of information a minute. This allows you to see what you want to see and process the information you need so that you don't get over-stimulated and overwhelmed by the information bombarding you.

Let's go back to the keys for a minute. When you program your mind to "see" that the keys are "lost" then the RAS begins to search for evidence to support that program. That's why your keys can be "lost" right in front of you. You may have even walked by the actual place where they are "lost", looked right at them and not seen them.

Now, if the brain can do that with keys, imagine what the brain can do with the concept of abundance.

Your RAS doesn't act alone like some random computer. It operates at your command. It's just that, for many of us, we forget or don't learn how to use this amazing feature of our mental "magic wand".

The RAS is truly the physical control center for deliberately creating magic.

Think about this. In times of great economic hardship, there have been people who have made great profits, even riches. What makes these people successful when others around them are seemingly suffering?

"I always tried to turn every disaster into an opportunity."
-John D. Rockefeller

"Opportunity often comes disguised in the form of misfortune, or temporary defeat."
-Napoleon Hill

Abundant people program themselves to see abundance and abundant opportunities around them all the time. When they are looking for their keys, they know they will be found, and often, they find an additional abundant opportunity or two while waiting for the keys to show up.

But, for most of us, learning to see abundance in every moment of life requires some remembering and re-training.

When we choose to incarnate, it is always a deliberate process. You are never forced to come to Earth against your will. You are not some hapless puppet of the Divine. You wanted to be here... especially at this time.

We are at an incredible time on this planet. Many Souls have chosen to be here at this time in order to serve God by deliberately carrying old conditioned patterns with the intention of being a part of clearing them in collective consciousness.

There is a massive army of Lightworkers on the planet right now who are re-learning to see Divine Abundance everywhere. Many of you have deliberately chosen a difficult life path so that you can be a part of creating a great return to Light in the collective consciousness.

So, if you have struggled with money, relationships, health, spirituality, life direction, abuse, trauma and shock, it is likely that you choose these struggles as catalysts to help you reprogram your mind to see abundance everywhere instead of lack.

Your Inner Wisdom attracted these circumstances to help you release the pattern and reclaim your Divine Heritage of abundance, not just for yourself but also for the entire body of humanity.

Think about this. Remember that vibrations modulate and affect each other. A low vibration can bring your vibration down and a high vibration can lift you up, provided there is resonance.

Collectively, our perception of the world is co-created by all of us on the planet. We have human beliefs about the earth we all share that create our collective way of seeing the world.

For example, we all believe that there is dirt of some sort, the sky is blue and that rain sometimes falls from the clouds. There are also a vast number of us who believe that the experience of lack, struggle and suffering are normal human conditions.

The way wealth is experienced on this planet is just the out-picturing of our collective consciousness. Most of the perceived wealth on this planet is experienced by a small percentage of humans living on earth. Truth be told, a majority of people on the planet are currently experiencing poverty.

Collective consciousness currently vibrates with lack.

But, consciousness is shifting and shifting quickly. In order to change our collective vibration, we have to change our individual vibration. All the pieces of the whole begin to add up.

When the vibrational shift reaches a critical mass, the abundance vibration will modulate the lack vibration and lift it up. This will happen first on an individual level, then on a community level, and ultimately on a collective level.

This is the most important thing we must do on the planet right now. We must individually restore old collective patterns of suffering and lack to their natural state of abundance.

That means that the most important thing you can do to help the planet right now is to take care of your individual abundance consciousness. This is the first step in fulfilling your life purpose as a Lightworker.

Once you consistently maintain an abundant vibration, you will, by Law of Attraction, attract to you relationships that are supportive and co-creative. From those relationships will come renewed abundant community consciousness.

These new abundant communities will then attract other

communities which seek to co-create. These communities will come together and make powerful abundant changes on a global level.

But, it has to start with you first. Everything you do, think and create is a metaphor for the state of consciousness of the whole Body of God. If you want to experience an abundant world, you have to start first with programming yourself to see the abundance that surrounds you constantly.

Programming your RAS to help you see the abundance is a vital step in aligning yourself with your abundant birthright. You will then see the abundance that is "hiding" right in front of you.

Exercises:

1. Begin each day with this affirmation. You can even write it down on an index card and take it with you to read several times a day. This will help reprogram your RAS and create new abundance thinking neuropathways:

God is my total fulfillment. God knows my needs and Desires before I am even conscious of them in my mind. Divine Mind knows all the perfect abundant answers for me. With God as my total fulfillment, all I have to do is know that I am always fully supported, deeply loved and magnificently powerful. My only job is to listen to my Inner Wisdom and take guided action. I relax knowing all the abundance I desire is right in front of me always.

You can shorten this statement simply to "God is my total fulfillment." Use this phrase when your old programs come up. Aligning with the energy of this phrase allows you to immediately know that there is an abundant solution at hand.

You just have to listen and wait.

Use this phrase, too, when it seems like things are not going according to "plan" and you are facing challenges. This will help you remember that, regardless of what the outer circumstances may look like, you are always in a state of being abundantly fulfilled.

2. Practice gratitude in all situations. Find what you love in every circumstance. Thinking gratefully automatically programs the RAS to find the things you love in a situation. Focusing on what you love creates more of what you love and before you know it, your situation has changed.

3. When you are facing a challenging situation, sit down, relax and see the desired end result in your minds eye. When you begin with the end in mind, you program the RAS to look for evidence to help bring the desired end into form.

Jesus said, "Blessed is the man who has suffered and found life."

-Thomas

Chapter Eleven

Creation is a Constantly Evolving Process. You are Always Doing it Right! You are Always Growing and Changing!

Focused Review:

Your thoughts and feelings create a vibration. Your vibration determines the experiences you "attract" into your life.

You are naturally abundant. Abundance is your natural vibration. Your creative powers work easily and effortlessly all the time. It is your job to direct them.

You are supported on your Earth Journey by specialized Loving Forces who guide you and give you information to keep you focused on the maximum expression of your soul.

Where you put your energy and attention is where you get growth in your life.

When you relax and trust the Creation Process, everything comes to you. It's a natural and daily process.

Gratitude and appreciation is a powerful creative vibration that helps you focus on what you want with delight.

Your Good Feelings show you that you are focusing on what you really want.

You are surrounded by Divine Siblings who seek to co-create with you. You are never alone.

The world is infinitely abundant. All you have to do is learn to see that it is everywhere.

You are always creating. Every moment your vibration is attuning to your reality. Creation happens whether you are conscious of it or not. It is your nature.

Creation is the natural state of the Divine. As representatives of the Divine we are constantly creating.

There is no real endpoint to creation. It's an ongoing, never-ending process. There is never a point when you just rest and cease to create. The minute you stop creating is the minute you cease to exist. You will not be living.

There are, of course, points of rest in the creative process. The energy of the Universe operates in pulses and waves, much like a heartbeat. But the heartbeat is continuous. The pulse of creation is eternal.

There is also no getting creation "right" or "wrong". It's all a process, subject to your co-creation. You can direct your experience within the flow of the process at all times with the option to change the direction at any given point.

The purpose of creation is to create. We are here to learn how to create in this dense dimension. When we are not in form, the flow of creation is easy. The conditioning field of this planet and the heaviness of the third dimension make deliberate creating more challenging here.

The endpoint, to a certain degree, is not so important. What is important is the degree to which you master the creative process. You are an "Earth Artist" and your job is to perfect the process of intentional creation.

Basically, that means that you can create what you want and if you don't like what you're creating you can change it. Your world is always giving you feedback about where you are on your creative journey. You have the power to change the direction at any given point.

Of course, your actions are always perfect. Inside the Body of God, there is no judgment. There are, however, consequences that manifest in kind in your outer reality.

If you are not applying the rules of creation in the direction in which you intend, your outer reality will show you where you need to "tweak" the process. If you are creating in a way that is not for the highest good of all, there will, at some point, be a natural consequence to your creation.

At this stage of our development, most of us go through a very natural process of "waking up" or remembering our creative potential. Over the last few years, the vibration of the awareness of this "waking up" process has been growing in dominance and more and more of us are remembering our natural creative power.

There are four different stages of remembering our creative consciousness:

Stage One: Unconscious Creation

In this phase of creative consciousness you are unaware of how your thoughts and vibrations create your experience. This level of consciousness is essentially creation by default.

Most of us start out in this phase of creative consciousness. Our earth experience supports our disconnection from the memory of our true creative potential. During this phase it is easy to perceive yourself as being a "victim" of your life, subject to the whims of fate.

Stage Two: You Create Your Own Reality

This phase marks the beginning of reclaiming your Divine Power. When you enter Stage Two, you begin to realize that your thoughts and emotions create your outer circumstances. What you think about and dream about comes about.

In Stage Two you make lists and vision boards to help you create what you want. You direct the creative process and the focus is "manifesting".

Stage Three: You Co-Create With God

In Stage Three you begin to realize that it isn't just your thinking alone that manifests your reality. After experimenting with Stage Two, you've probably realized that "magic" and miracles happen. Manifestation often occurs in ways that go beyond what your mind thought you could create.

Thoughts and inspirations about "how" to create the things and situations you desire happen spontaneously and often without a lot of conscious intention.

Things are "better than you thought" and you realize that a higher force is working with you to help you create. And the things you desire to create often have far-reaching positive effects for many people.

Stage Four: You Are The Divine Flow Of Abundance

Staying consistently in Stage Four of creation is a little challenging. Most of us will have flashes of Stage Four but to maintain this stage consistently is difficult unless you completely divorce yourself from the "real" world. This is why Enlightened Masters who spend years away from people and civilization can achieve this stage of creation more easily.

In Stage Four you are so deeply aligned in consciousness with abundance that all your thoughts, inspirations, desires and actions are abundant. You know no lack. All your needs are met, even anticipated before you have them. You become the perfect vehicle for the Divine.

You are in flow. You are the flow and you expect and align with perfect support.

The reality is that we are all always in Stage Four. We just aren't always conscious of it. But the magnificence of this system of remembering is that each stage is the perfect catalyst for your growth and expansion into the next stage.

In Stage One, we struggle and get frustrated with life. Things seem to operate by whim or fate. You feel out of control and even scared about your life and your future. The frustration and the fear are the perfect catalysts to help you deepen your desire to "find a better way".

Think about this for a minute. What experience or feelings did you have to start you on your path to discovering the idea that your thoughts create your reality? Whatever it was, your amazing Self created that situation to help you remember Stage Two of creation.

As you evolve through Stage Two, as you experience more and more success at manifesting the experiences you desire, your Desires get bigger and bigger. Pretty soon you are intending things that your mind simply does not know "how" to make happen and you realize that something bigger and more unlimited than your perception has to "step in" to make your Desires manifest.

Trusting in the "something bigger" is the beginning of Stage Three. Now you are taking bigger and bigger leaps of faith and letting go of the worry that you don't know "how" to make something happen.

As you trust and relax into your expanded nature and your Divinity, your experiences become more and more abundant. You raise your baseline vibrational frequency and your experience of life feels better.

As you take bigger leaps of faith and deepen your creative awareness, you gradually move into a space of recognizing that you don't have to consciously manifest a specific outer reality but that, instead, all you have to do is to become conscious of the Divine manifested as you and that that consciousness, in and of itself, is the source of your abundance and supply.

In other words, the more you recognize that you are a cell within the Body of God and that, by nature, you are the abundance of the Divine...always...the more you simply live out that abundance.

The truth is, we don't have to walk around consciously manifesting things. But we have to go through these steps in order to reawaken our natural abundant consciousness and to work around our neurobiology and conditioning.

Our biology demands consistent duplicatable experiences to verify and validate our beliefs and consequently our experiences. This consistency protects us and allows us to predict the results of our actions.

The more consistent our experiences, the more we come to expect them. The more we come to expect them, the more likely it is that they will come into form.

As you can see, this is a perfect process and you absolutely can't get it wrong!

Every step of creation, including the frustration, the pain and sometimes feeling out of control, is a perfect part of the reawakening process. Your "negative" experiences only serve to deepen your Desires and clarify your intentions.

It's never really about the end result. The things or even experiences we are seeking to manifest are simply vehicles for our consciousness to measure finite, third dimensional proof of where we are at with our vibration. We need to start the process of remembering our creative power by manifesting "things" because this is a "thing"-based reality.

The real goal is to become manifested Divine Consciousness. Ultimately, the things are just an outer effect. In theory, as we progress collectively through these phases, we could live abundance in form without "things", if we choose. We could also instantly manifest "things" seemingly out of thin air, if we choose.

But in the meantime, we are having a great time going through the process of waking up to our creative power and potential. You are an expansive, ever-evolving, growing and changing individuated aspect of the Divine.

Your life is a creative adventure! Stay focused on the goal of remembering your creative potential and embark on each day like the grand creative Divine Adventurer you are!

Remember, you're always doing it right!

You can't get it wrong.

Exercises:

1. In your meditation this week, imagine yourself resting quietly in the palm of God. You are fully supported and you can simply relax in the Hand of God knowing that the Laws of the Universe serve you.

2. Evaluate what stage of creation you are in. Ask your Inner

Wisdom how you can deepen your awareness and understanding of the stage that you are in. Are you willing to create bigger things and take greater leaps of faith? How can you deepen and enjoy your Earth Adventure even more?

3. If you are experiencing frustration or fear regarding your intentions, what are your feelings trying to tell you? What intentions and Desires are you deepening? What clarity is this feedback giving you?

Jesus said, "It is impossible for a man to mount two horses or to stretch two bows. And it is impossible for a servant to serve two masters; otherwise he will honor the one and treat the other contemptuously. New wine is not put into old wineskins, lest they burst; nor is old wine put into a new wineskin, lest it spoil it. An old patch is not sewn into a new garment, because a tear would result."

-Thomas

Chapter Twelve

You Take Guided Actions That are in Alignment with Your Desires and Beliefs.

Focused Review:

Your thoughts and feelings create a vibration. Your vibration determines the experiences you "attract" into your life.

You are naturally abundant. Abundance is your natural vibration. Your creative powers work easily and effortlessly all the time. It is your job to direct them.

You are supported on your Earth Journey by specialized Loving Forces who guide you and give you information to keep you focused on the maximum expression of your soul.

Where you put your energy and attention is where you get growth in your life.

When you relax and trust the Creation Process, everything comes to you. It's a natural and daily process.

Gratitude and appreciation are powerful creative vibrations that help you focus on what you want with delight.

Your Good Feelings show you that you are focusing on what you really want.

You are surrounded by Divine Siblings who seek to co-create with you. You are never alone.
The world is infinitely abundant. All you have to do is learn to see that it is everywhere.
The purpose of your creative efforts is to grow your conscious capacity to create. Everything you experience is perfect and helping you deepen your creative abilities.

You intended to incarnate on Earth at this time. Earth is a very special place where creation happens third dimensionally. That means that we have form, time and space.

When we are not in form, creation can happen etherically. But in form, we have to learn how to use the same skills that are so natural to us, in the thick, heaviness of third dimensional life.

In other words, we have to "do", in addition to "being" in order to create.

Let me first start by stating that, according to Universal Law, it is theoretically possible to manifest out of thin air. There are many stories of saints and adepts who can do this.

But, as you just learned, most of us are in Stage Two of creation and manifesting an apple out of thin air is much more difficult than going to the grocery store and simply buying one.

For most of us, manifesting an experience requires corresponding actions in order for creation to take place. Action is a vital step that can be deeply misunderstood.

We live in an action-based world with deep action-oriented belief systems. We do, do, and do. And many of us have strong beliefs that our abundance is attached to our doing.

Think about this for a minute. Do you believe that you have to work to make money? This is a very common action-based belief. The reality of abundance consciousness is that money, the collectively agreed upon outer effect of abundance, can easily show up in your life without work. Do you know people who are financially wealthy who have not worked for their money? (Trust me, they are out there.)

In order to properly apply action you have to define what action is. Action can be defined as doing something for a particular purpose even though we often describe it as activity, force or energy.

If action is doing something for a particular purpose then the steps we take to align our vibrations can be deemed as action. Meditation is action. So is day dreaming, imagining, visualizing, praying and tending to your mindset.

Before the action of "doing" happens, the steps necessary to create the inspiration and vibration aligned with the intention have to happen first. In other words, before you go out and make something happen, make sure that your energy is aligned.

Creating vibrational alignment is the action that has to be taken prior to any other actions, otherwise you will be using sheer force of will to try and make something happen. And, as you probably know from experience, using sheer will is not sustainable, nor is it energizing or fruitful.

We are so deeply conditioned to "do" without lining up the energies first. Because we are so deeply conditioned to believe that our abundance is tied to our doing, most of us are out doing and doing and doing in the hopes that one of the many things we are trying to do will yield the desired results.

Generally speaking, these kinds of actions leave us exhausted, burned out and frustrated. (But, of course, these emotions are helping you clarify your intentions and deepening your desire to do things in a different and more effective way.)

How much of what you are doing is actually tied to your dreams and what you are intending? Your actions, being a form of attention, partly determine what you create. Where you spend your time and energy is where you get growth.

If you are intending to be a good parent who is totally present and available to your children but the only time you spend with them is kissing them goodnight after a long day at work, your actions are not lined up with your intentions. It's like trying to ride two horses at the same time.

It is very possible that you are in a job situation that is so busy that, for now, you only have the time to kiss them goodnight. But, if you intend to change that, you must also take the time to line up your vibration with the change you desire.

For example, you might take two minutes every hour to focus on your children's photos at your desk and imagine a lifestyle where you get to spend lots of time playing with your family.

Realistically evaluating your lifestyle might also give you options to change your actions and bring them more into alignment with your intentions. For example, are you using your time doing other things when you could be spending time with your family? When the phone rings during family time, do you answer it and start a conversation with someone who is lower down on your list of important people just to be "polite"?

Here's another example. Let's say you intend to become a best-selling author. In order to do that you must first write a book, unless, of course you are also manifesting a ghostwriter. Even then, you have to have a topic and some research.

Yet, how often does the desire to write a book stay a dream? The actions have to happen to bring the book into form. You can write a book (albeit slowly) in just 10 minutes a day.

And, even if you don't quite know what to write yet, you can still design your book cover, investigate getting published, read other similar books, play with outlines, day dream about being on Oprah and imagine your book at the top of the New York Times

Bestseller list. You can do this while riding the bus or subway.

If you are not taking the appropriate actions to create your Desires, it's usually only for two reasons:

1. What you are intending isn't really a pure heart's Desire.
2. You have limiting beliefs that are keeping you from believing in your success.

The lack of action and obvious lack of results is simply the Bigger You showing you that you're not on target. If you're not doing what needs to be done then as a creative genius, you know that it's time to go back to your meditation chair and ask yourself what is really going on.

If what you are intending, but not aligning with, isn't really what you want, it's crucial that you ask yourself some serious and self-loving questions. Sometimes the desires we have are close to what we want but something is off. Often the desire is based on what we think is "possible" or what we "should" do, not what we really want.

Remember, in order for creation to work, the Desire has to be a pure heart's Desire. It has to really turn you on. That energy of being "turned on" is the catalyst for right action that lines you up with your intention.

If you have limiting beliefs that are keeping you from taking right action, it's crucial that you set the intention to clear them up. You are only going to take right action to the degree to which you believe that you can have what you desire. If you believe you can't have it, you won't do what is necessary.

If you don't believe that you can have what you intend, then your outer reality will clearly demonstrate that belief to you in every arena in your life. Everything you see, hear, smell, touch and taste is an out-picturing of your inner belief system.

Your outer world is really just a metaphor or a story of your inner world. You can look to the "story of your life" to find the limiting belief that may be keeping you from taking right action.

For example, let's say that you are challenged with direction and you always get lost. Getting "lost" is a metaphor for not being on target with your intended creation. You know where you are headed but you're not taking the right "steps" to get there. You're lacking "direction" in your life.

Or maybe the brakes in your car aren't working. Maybe you are going so "fast" that you're missing important details. Perhaps you need a "break", some time for self-renewal and nurturing.

There are two things you can do when you identify the blocks that are keeping you from taking action. It is helpful to do both. First, you must work on your inner mindset and beliefs. There are many, many wonderful block removing techniques available to us at this time.

I personally recommend The Emotional Freedom Techniques (EFT) because it is fast, quick, and easy to learn and do, but I encourage you to find a strategy that you are vibrationally aligned with. Some of you may need a coach or a therapist to help you move past your blocks. Trust yourself and go with a strategy that feels right to you.

Remember, once you set the intention, your outer reality will bring you the answers you need.

In addition to working on re-aligning your belief system with your natural abundance, you can also change your outer reality to influence your inner reality. Think about it. You know how hard it can be sometimes to change your mind. Working on the outer reality to change the metaphor can be a powerful way to influence your inner thinking.

Here is an example. I had a friend who was feeling "lost" in her life. She lived with me for a year while she got back on her feet following a divorce. My house was close to a beautiful lake with a nice trail around it.

The first few days after she moved in, my friend drove to the lake, parked her car and walked around the three-mile path. On the first day, she was gone for over three hours on her three-mile walk. When she returned she reported that she had "lost" her car and couldn't remember where she had parked it so she walked around and around the lake trying to find her car.

The next time she headed for the lake she was determined to remember where she had parked her car but she, again, lost her car and was gone for hours. This happened a couple more times until finally she asked for help.

I suggested that she tie a huge neon green scarf to her car antenna so that when she came around the full circle of the lake the scarf would be vibrantly flapping in the wind and showing her where she parked.

It worked! The change in the story marked a real shift in my friend's journey to "find" herself and her direction. Changing her outer reality symbolically created the energy for her to also change her inner thinking and beliefs.

Life is intended to be easy and effortless. We are deeply conditioned to push past resistance and "do it anyway". But when you understand the principles of creation, you know that resistance is a message from your Inner Wisdom helping you clarify your Desire and intent.

If you are avoiding action because it doesn't feel good, dive in and ask yourself this important question: "What Do I Want?"

Simply focusing your attention in the direction of what you want and away from the frustration and resistance can help you get your energy back for creating. If you are digging deep and struggling to push yourself into taking an action that you resist, pushing harder might create results in the short run, but they won't create long-term abundance.

When you line up your energy and then take guided actions that are in alignment with your intentions, the "doing" seems effortless and magical. When you align your energy, really feel and see your intention as already coming true, then you allow a flow of energy that is bigger than you by yourself, pushing and struggling to make something happen.

Exercises:

1. Keep a log of how you are spending your time for one week. Evaluate your intentions for your life and ask yourself if your actions reflect your intentions.   Are you doing the things necessary to create what you really want in your life?

2. If your actions are not in alignment with your Desires and beliefs ask yourself if you are really wanting what you are intending. The truth always creates!

3. Do you have limiting beliefs that are keeping you from taking actions that are in alignment with your Desires? If so, how are these beliefs demonstrating themselves in your outer reality? How can you change the metaphor in your outer reality?

4. How you eat dinner is a metaphor for how you nurture and nourish yourself. Make a point to fix yourself a really nice nutritious meal and sit down and have a lovely dinner with yourself or your friends and family.

5. Make a list of one thing you can do each day to bring you closer to your intention. Remember, sometimes action is as simple as sitting in your chair and daydreaming for five minutes.

"You are fully supported, deeply loved and magnificently powerful. You are an unlimited Child of the Universe."

-**Thomas**

About the Author

Karen Curry is an entrepreneur, teacher, mentor, coach and author. She is the founder of The Prosperity Revolution and deeply dedicated to sharing and co-creating an abundant global community.

Karen is also the author of *The Prosperity Revolution, EFT for Parents,* and *Waging Peace in the Face of Rage* and weekly articles about abundance and spirituality. She is the host of the internationally acclaimed radio show, Prosperity Radio.

Karen's websites include:
www.humandesignforeveryone.com
www.indigoheartpublishing.com
www.joyfulmission.com

Karen is available for private consultations, keynote talks and to conduct in-house seminars and workshops. You can reach her at karen@joyfulmission.com or call 832-928-5110.

How to Buy Copies of this Book and Other Books and Reports:

You may buy copies of this book, and others by the same author for you, for yourself and friends in the following formats:

- Paperback

- E-book (immediate download)

- Audio (coming soon!)

The easiest way to get your copy is visit Karen's website at www.indigoheartpublishing.com and click on the bookstore link. From there you will be directed to your choice books and reports in your choice format and purchase option.

For bulk orders and book club purchases, call 832-928-5110.

Publishers: The goal is to have this book in over 30 languages covering 97% of the world, and over 500 million readers. We are still looking for suitable publishers in specific countries to keep extending its availability worldwide in various languages. Interested publishers please call 832-928-5110.

Published by:

Indigo Heart Publishing
200 E. Rainbow Ridge
The Woodlands, Texas 77381
832-928-5110
www.indigoheartpublishing.com